RICHARD SCARRY'S
Best Busytown
Games &
Activity Book

STERLING CHILDREN'S BOOKS
New York

STERLING CHILDREN'S BOOKS
New York

An Imprint of Sterling Publishing
387 Park Avenue South
New York, NY 10016

ISBN 978-1-4027-7315-0

Published in 2013 by Sterling Publishing Co, Inc.
By arrangement with J B Publishing, Inc.
On behalf of the Richard Scarry Corporation

New illustrations by Huck Scarry

Designed by Matthew Rossetti

Distributed in Canada by Sterling Publishing
c/o Canadian Manda Group, 165 Dufferin Street
Toronto, Onatrio, Canada M6K 3H6
Distributed in the United Kingdom by GMC Distribution Services
Castle Place, 166 High Street, Lewes, East Sussex, England BN7 1XU
Distributed in Australia by Capricorn Link (Australia) Pty. Ltd.
P.O. Box 704, Windsor, NSW 2756, Australia

 a J R Sansevere • J B Publishing Book

For information about custom editions, special sales, premium and corporate purchases, please contact
Sterling Special Sales Department at 800-805-5489 or specialsales@sterlingpublishing.com.

Manufactured in China
Lot #:
2 4 6 8 10 9 7 5 3 1
12/12

www.sterlingpublishing.com/kids

Up, Up, and Away!

Huckle and Lowly are ready to go, go, go! Connect the dots from 1 to 32 to help them get off the ground! Then color the picture.

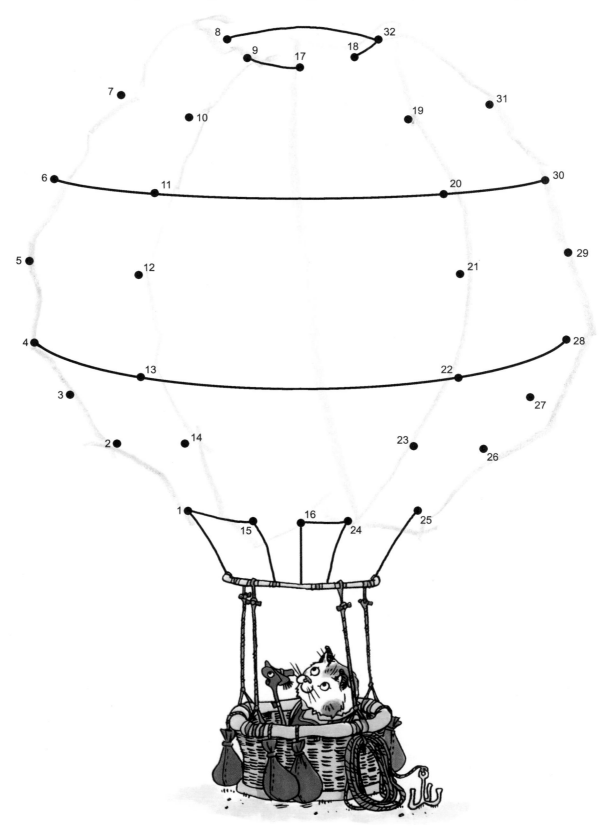

An Airborne Adventure!

Zip! Zoom! Huckle and Sally are flying! Help them soar through the busy sky and land safely on the runway. Don't forget to keep your seat belts fastened!

START!

DRINK WATER

FINISH!

2

5

Let's Go to the Air Show

Everyone loves to go to the air show to see all of the old-fashioned airplanes. Can you find the 8 ways the picture on the right is different from the one on the left? Of course you can!

Bicycle Search

Skip loves to ride his bike. *Look out, Huckle!* Find the bicycle-themed words from the Word Bank hidden in the puzzle below. Look across and down!

Word Bank

BELL
BIKE
HELMET
HORN
PEDAL
RACE
RIDE
ROAD
SAFETY

```
H  E  L  M  E  T
O  B  I  P  C  S
R  A  C  E  R  A
N  Y  C  D  I  F
L  R  O  A  D  E
B  E  L  L  E  T
E  B  I  K  E  Y
```

Let's Roll!

Where is everybody off to? Color all of the letters that spell
B-I-K-E in the puzzle below. Then write the uncolored
letters on the line below to reveal the answer.

B P I L A K

Y E G R B O

I U K N E D

What does it say?

_____

Two-Wheeler

Bridget is showing off her new scooter. Can you find the two pictures that look exactly alike?

Roadwork

Oh, no! Huckle and Lowly are trying to ride to the ice-cream shop, but the road needs to be fixed first. Can you draw these 2 pieces of road in the right place and direction to complete the pathway for them?

What Doesn't Belong?

It's Arthur's job to pack the basket for the Pig family's picnic. Help him out by drawing an X over the things that don't belong in the basket.

Picnic Panic!

Oh, no! The ants are going to ruin the Pig family's picnic lunch!
Save the day by finding all 10 ants in the scene below.

Camping Crossword

Huckle and his friends are going camping! Use the picture clues to fill in the puzzle below. Look at the word list if you need help. Happy camping!

1) down

1) across

2) across

3) across

3) down

5) across

4) down

6) across

Word Bank

BEAR	**LANTERN**
FIRE	**LOGS**
FOREST	**SKUNK**
HIKE	**TENT**

Who's There?

Camping in the woods is fun, but there are a lot of strange noises at night.
Connect the dots from 1 to 40 to see who woke Ella up. Then color the picture.

Stinky Skunk

Tear the **red deck** of cards out of the back of this book and
play the Stinky Skunk game with Huckle and his friends!

Object of the Game
Be the player with the most matching
pairs of cards. If you're left holding
the Stinky Skunk card, you lose!

Huckle
Cat

Bridget
Murphy

Arthur
Pig

Stinky
Skunk

Setting Up
This game is for 2 to 4 players.
The **red deck** contains 32 character
cards and 1 Stinky Skunk card.

1) Shuffle the cards.
2) Deal the cards one at a time till
   they are all gone.

How Do You Play?
1) Look at your cards. Remove all of the matching pairs and place them
   face up in front of you.

2) The player to the left of the dealer holds his cards out to the player on his
   left, so that only backs are visible.

3) This player takes one card from the
   offered cards. If a pair is made, it is
   placed faceup on the table.

4) This player then offers his cards to the
   player to his left and so on.

5) Play continues until all pairs have been
   made. One player will be left holding
   the Stinky Skunk card.

Huckle
Cat

Huckle
Cat

Stinky
Skunk

How Do You Win?
The player with the most pairs wins the game!

Hide-and-Seek!

You can play the Hide-and-Seek game with these cards, too. Here's how!

Object of the Game
Be the player to find the most pairs of hiding campers.

Stinky Skunk

Setting Up
This game is for 1 to 4 players.
1) Remove the Stinky Skunk card from the deck.
2) Shuffle the cards.
3) Place the cards facedown in a grid:

How Do You Play?
1) Once all of the cards have been laid out, the player to the left of the dealer goes first. He turns over 2 cards.

2) If the cards match, take the pair and take another turn. Each time you make a match, take another turn. If the cards do not match, flip them back over. Then it is the next player's turn.

3) Keep going until all cards have been paired up.

How Do You Win?
The player who has the most pairs of cards wins the game!

Lost!

Uh-oh! These campers were searching for firewood when they lost their way. Help them find their way through the woods back to camp. You can do it!

START!

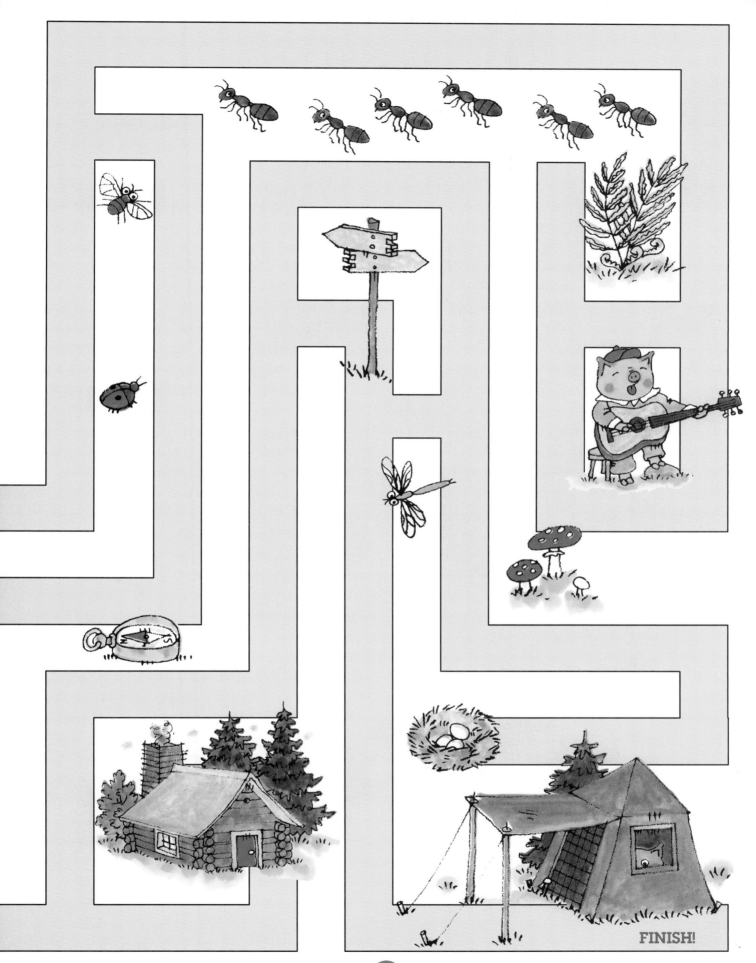

FINISH!

Go, Huckle, Go!

Today is Race Day! Huckle has his truck all ready to go!
Find the 2 pictures below that look exactly alike.

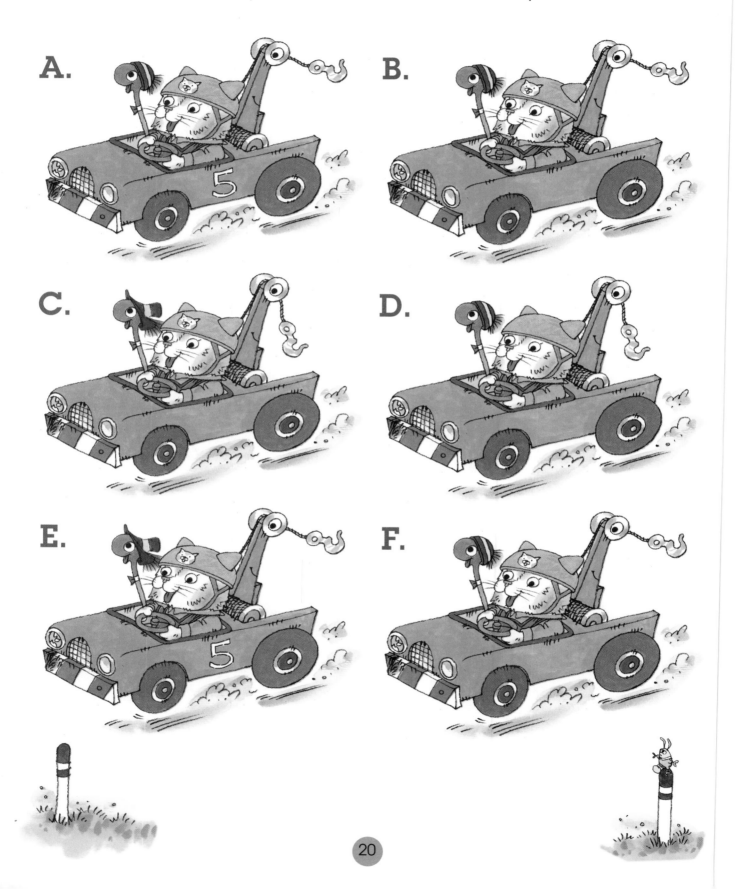

A.

B.

C.

D.

E.

F.

Busytown Race Game

These are the rules and instructions for the board game on the next two pages. You can keep the game board inside the book, or tear the pages out along the perforations and tape them together.

Object of the Game
Guide Huckle and his friends around the racetrack to the finish line.

Setting Up
- 2 to 4 players
- 4 coins (any kind will do!)
- A game piece for each player (cut these out from page 96)

How Do You Play?

1) Each player drops the 4 coins. The one with the greatest number of heads goes first, the second-greatest number of heads goes second, and so on. Each player puts his game token on the starting line.

2) When it is your turn, drop the 4 coins. The number of heads you get is the number of spaces you can move your game piece toward the finish line.

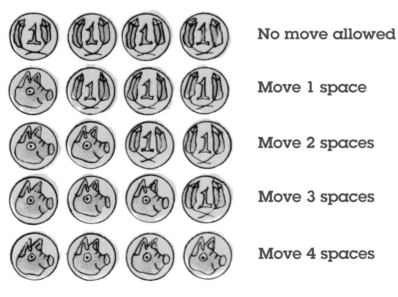

No move allowed

Move 1 space

Move 2 spaces

Move 3 spaces

Move 4 spaces

3) When you land on a space with writing on it, do what it says.

When you're ready to play, turn the page and go, go, go!

How Do You Win?
The first player to make it to the finish line wins the race!

21

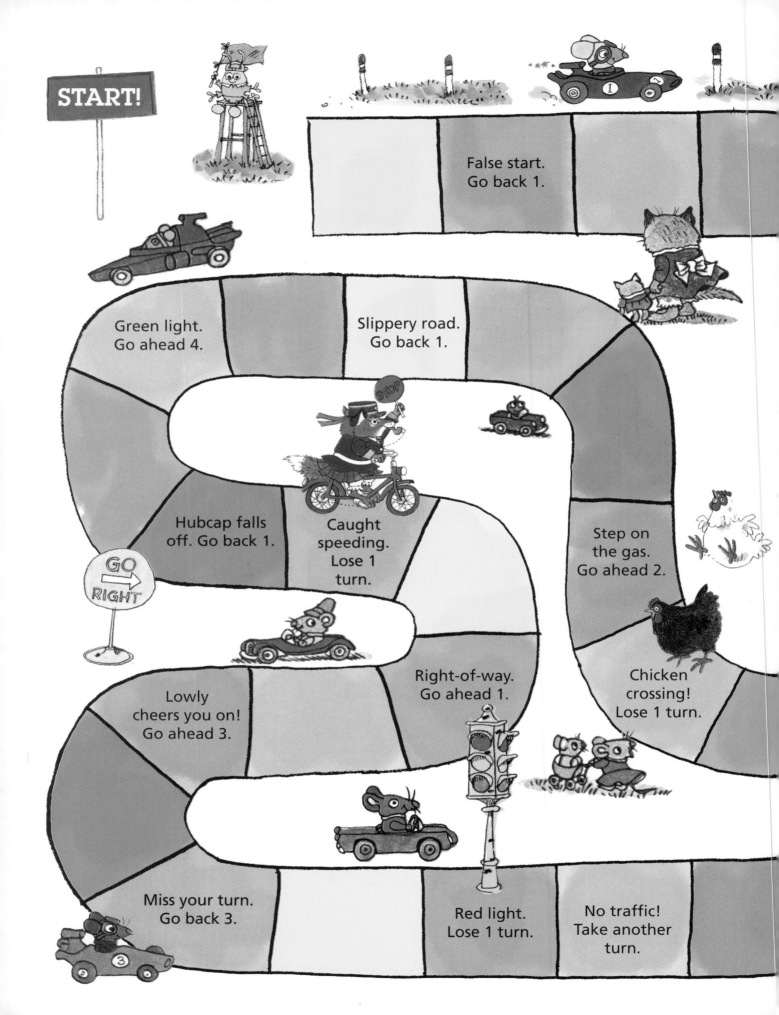

Red Light, Green Light

Can you help Bridget get through the maze of traffic lights below? Make a path that alternates from red light 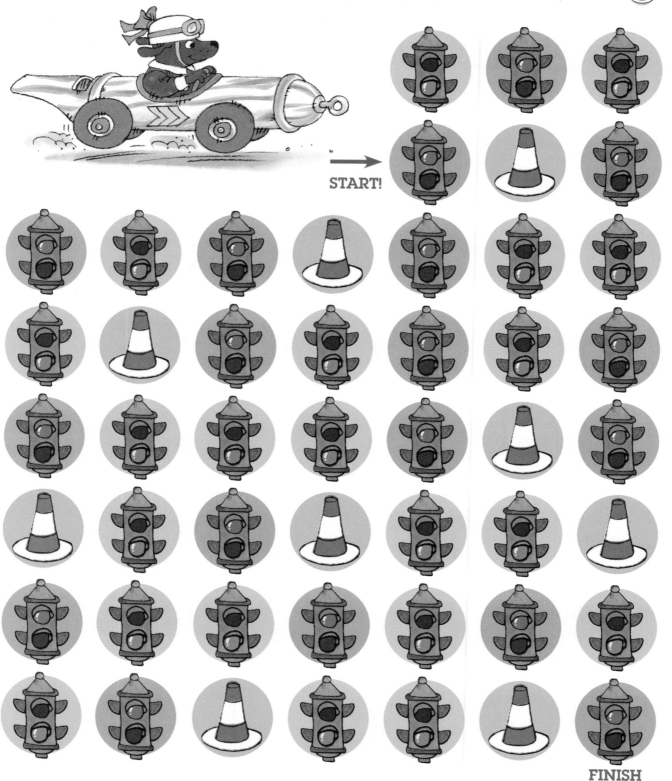 to green light. You can move up and down or left to right, but not diagonally. Try not to hit any cones !

START!

FINISH

What Comes Next?

Circle the car in the box at the end of each row that completes the pattern.

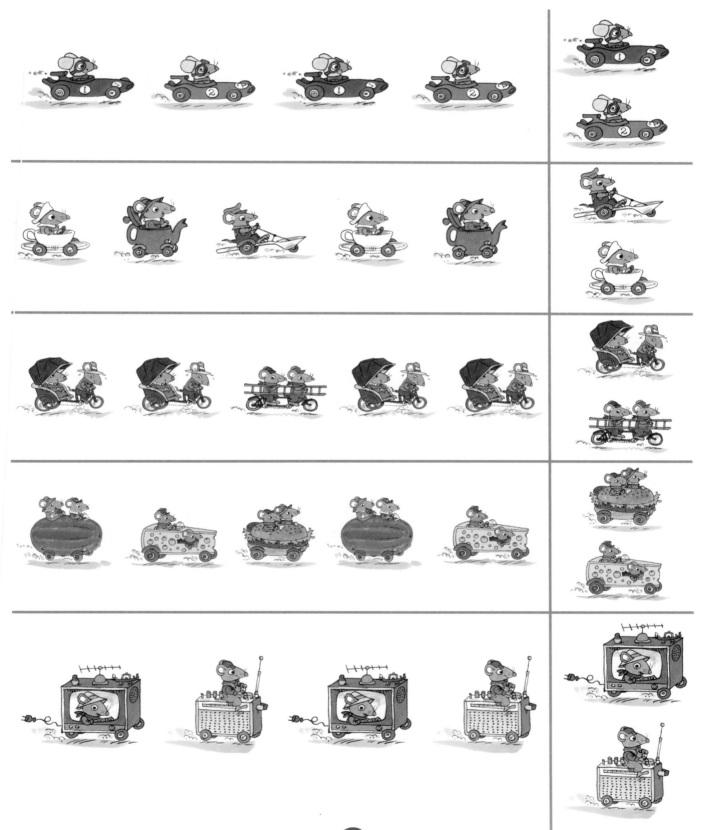

Let's Go to the Museum

Oh boy! Huckle, Sally and Mother Cat are taking a taxi to the museum.
Help them find their way through Busytown.

START!

MUSEUM

FINISH

Fossil Find

Uh-oh! The dinosaur bones at the museum got all mixed up! Can you help Lowly find the one bone below that doesn't have a match? Thank you!

Let's Color

Huckle and Lowly like to visit the Egyptian exhibit at the museum.
Color in the picture of the mummy below.

Sandbox Search

Huckle and Skip are having fun playing in the sand. Find the sandbox-themed words from the Word Bank hidden in the puzzle below. Look across and down!

Word Bank

CARS
DIG
PAIL
PLAY
ROCKS
SAND
SHOVEL
TRUCKS

T	R	O	C	K	S
R	D	I	G	P	H
U	S	X	C	L	O
C	A	R	S	A	V
K	N	N	I	Y	E
S	D	P	A	I	L

Fun and Games

The children love to play all kinds of games. Use the picture clues to fill in the puzzle below. Look at the word list if you need help.

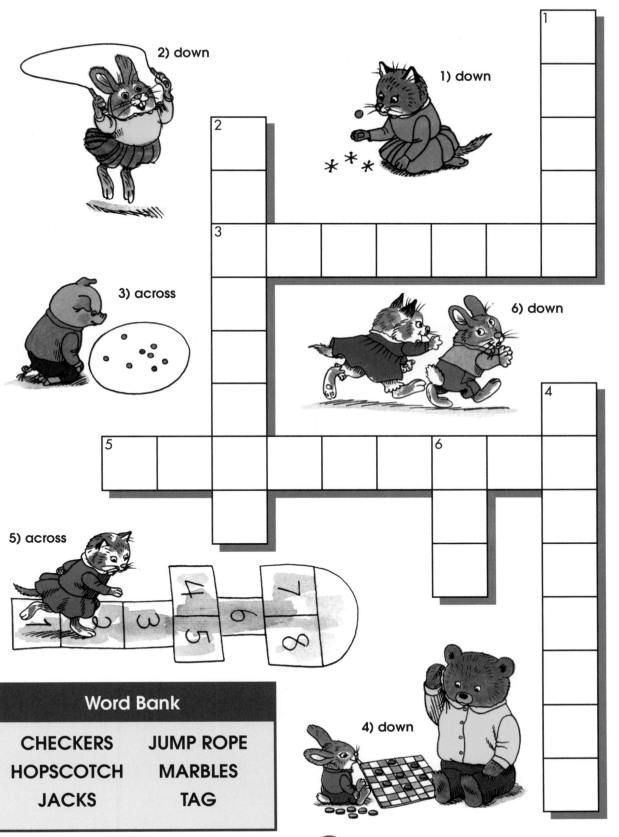

2) down

1) down

2

3

3) across

6) down

4

5

6

5) across

4) down

Word Bank

CHECKERS   JUMP ROPE

HOPSCOTCH   MARBLES

JACKS   TAG

A Fair Day

It's a great day to go to the Busytown fair. Can you find the 8 ways the picture on the right is different from the one on the left?

Color-By-Number

What prize did Skip win for Bridget at the fair? Fill in each numbered space with the correct color to find out.

1 = yellow

2 = blue

3 = red

4 = green

5 = brown

6 = black

Mirror, Mirror

Huckle and Lowly are in the funhouse. Draw how their reflections appear in the crazy mirror! They might look tall and thin or short and squat.
Then color the picture.

Summertime

Summer is here! There are 6 things that don't belong in this scene. Draw a circle around each one.

What Comes Next?

Draw a line from the dot at the end of each line to the shape that comes next in the pattern. Lowly did the first one for you. Thanks, Lowly!

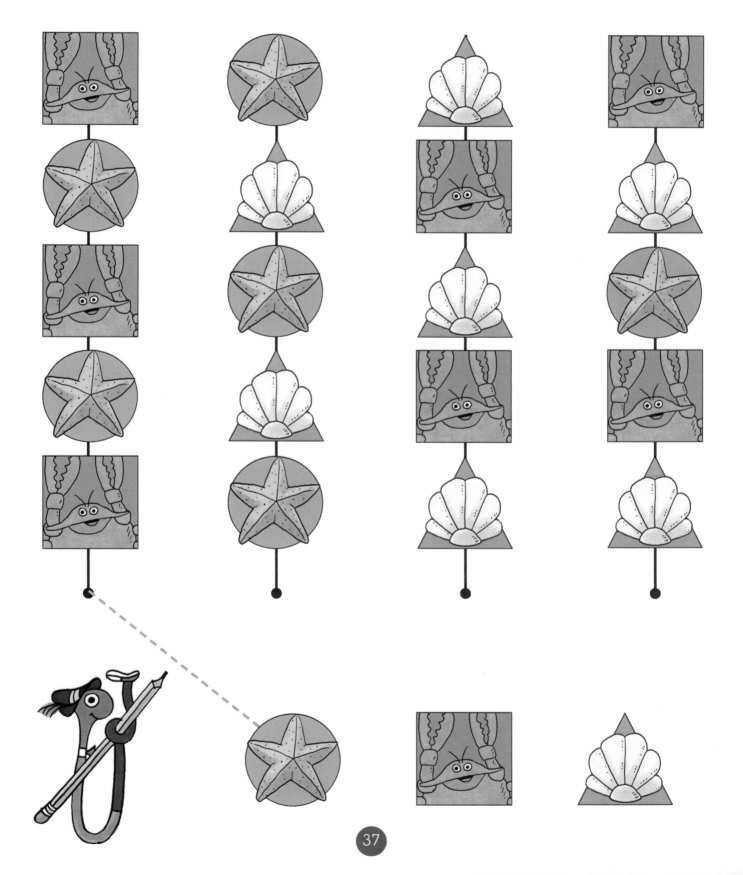

Let's Go to the Seashore

What a great day for the beach! Fill in the puzzle below using the picture clues. Use the Word Bank if you need help.

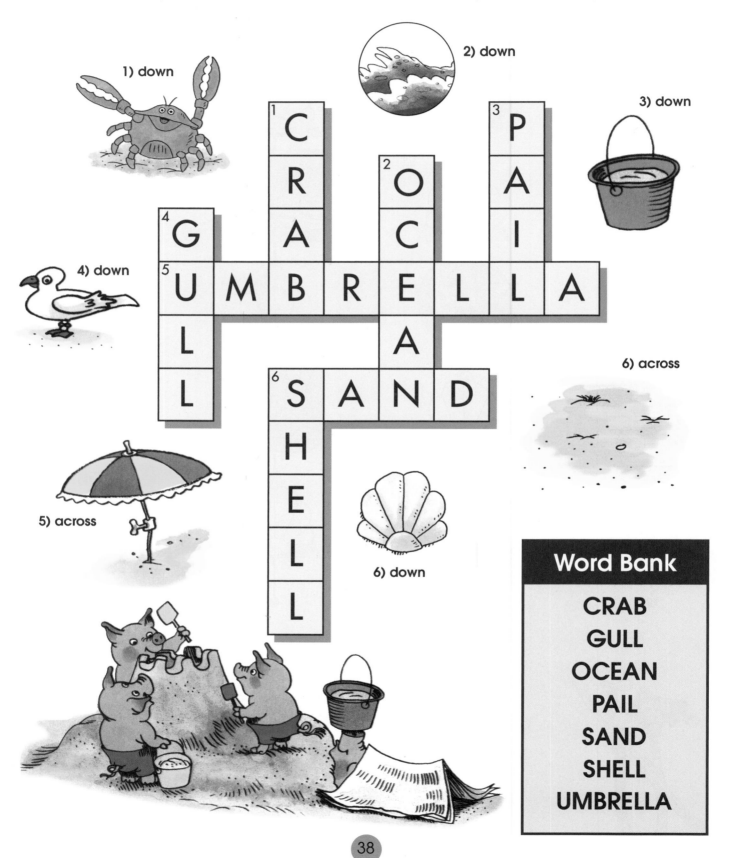

1) down

2) down

3) down

4) down

5) across

6) across

6) down

Word Bank

CRAB
GULL
OCEAN
PAIL
SAND
SHELL
UMBRELLA

Beach Bug

See what Goldbug has built in the sand by connecting the dots from 1 to 33. Then color the picture.

Beachcomber

Object of the Game
Try to form boxes by connecting dots.

Setting Up
This game is for 2 to 4 players. Each player should have a different colored pen or crayon.

How Do You Play?
1) Each player takes a turn connecting 2 neighboring dots with a straight line. You can go up and down and side to side, but not diagonally.

2) Try to be the player who makes a box by adding the last line of a square. When you do, write your initial in the box and take another turn. Each plain square is worth 1 point, each shell is worth 2 points, and each starfish is worth 3 points!

How Do You Win?
The player with the most points wins!

2 points **3 points**

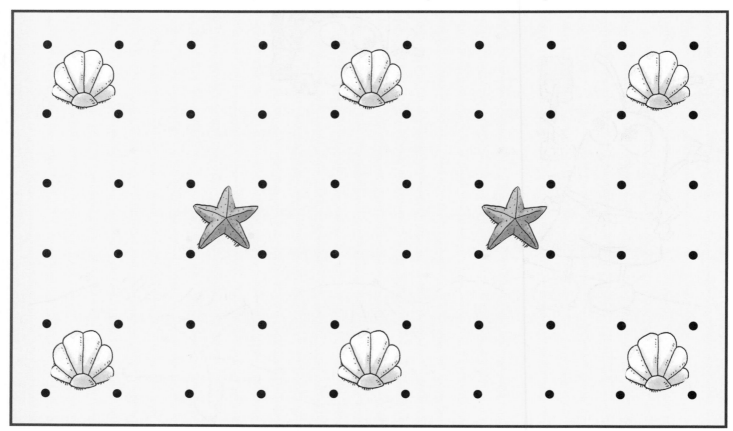

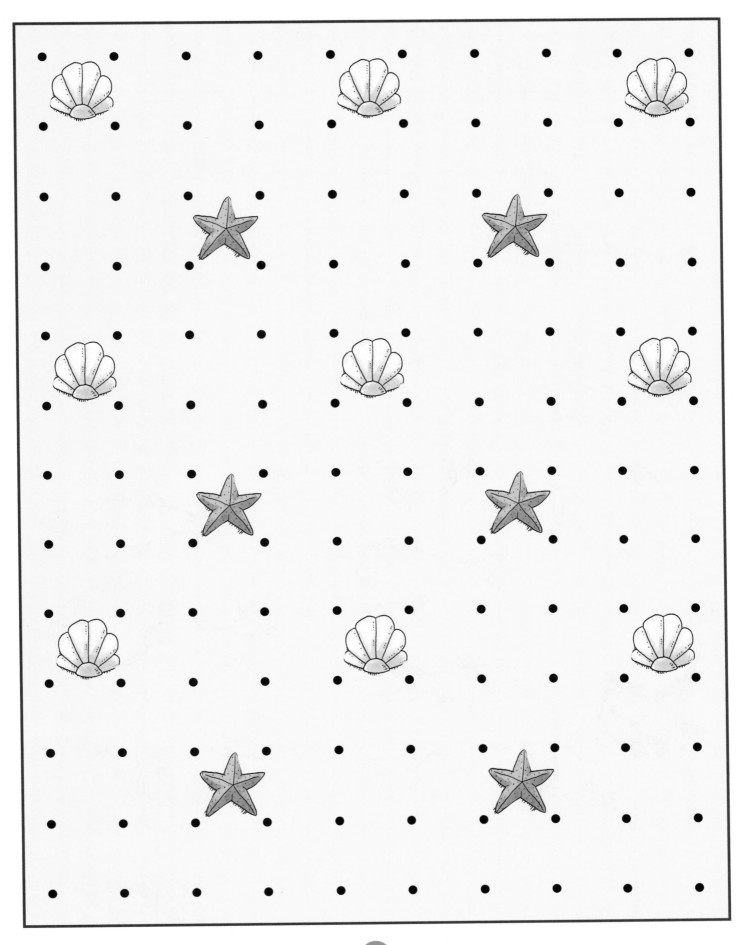

Sea Search

Huckle and Lowly are snorkeling. Help them find two fish that do not match any of the others.

Marine Mystery

What did Huckle see underwater? Color the letters found in the word **D-I-V-E** each time they appear, and the remaining letters will reveal the answer. Then draw what he saw in the space below the puzzle!

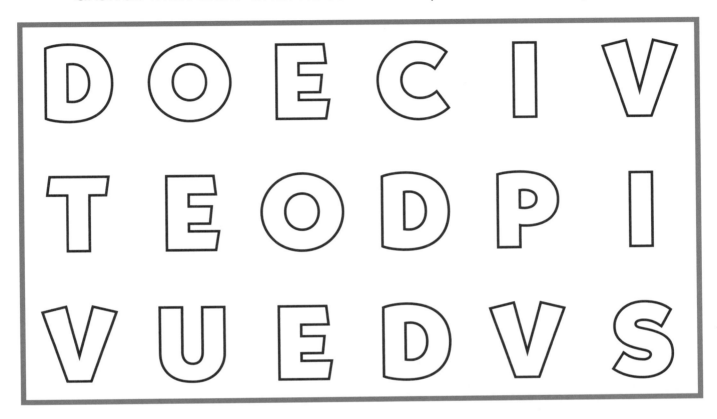

D O E C I V
T E O D P I
V U E D V S

Seaside Scene

Complete the beach scene below by writing the number of each missing piece into the correct empty space. The first one is done for you.

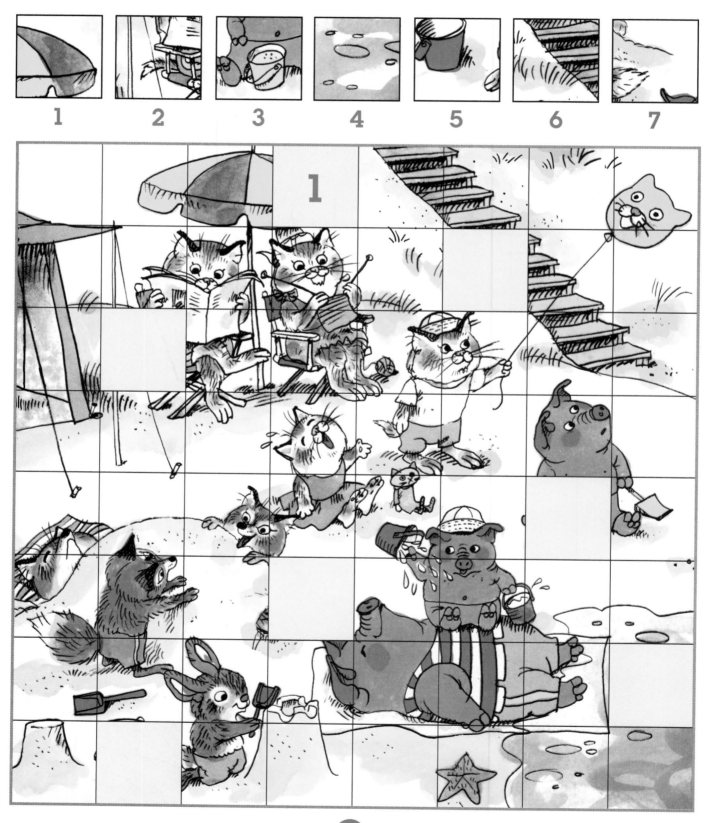

Tacklebox Tangle

Uh-oh! The three fishermen got their lines all tangled up!
Trace each line to find out who caught which object.

Go Fish!

Huckle loves to go fishing. Tear the **blue deck** of cards out of the back of this book, you can come along!

Object of the Game
Be the player who collects the most sets of cards.

Setting Up
- This game is for 2 to 4 players.
- The blue deck contains 36 cards (9 sets of 4 cards each.)

- Shuffle the cards.
- The dealer deals 5 cards to each player.
- Place the rest of the deck facedown in the center of the table as the draw pile.

big fish

old boot

rusty anchor

tin can

How Do You Play?
1) On his turn, a player asks one the other players if he has a particular type of card. You can only ask for cards that you already have in your hand.

2) If the player who was asked has the card, he must give it up. If he has more than one, he must give those up too.

Do you have any anchors?

3) The asking player's turn continues until he does not get any more cards.

4) When a player does not have the card that was asked for, he must tell the other player to "Go Fish!"

5) The asking player must then take a card from the draw pile. The game continues with the next player to the left.

6) When a player collects all 4 cards of a type, he has made a set. He then lays the set in front of him.

7) Keep playing until all cards are gone from the draw pile. Reshuffle the draw pile, if necessary.

How Do You Win?
Be the player with the most sets at the end of the game!

Sports Stuff

Huckle and his friends love to play all kinds of sports.
Can you find the group of balls that has the exact same
number and kind of balls as the bag Huckle is holding?

A.

B.

C.
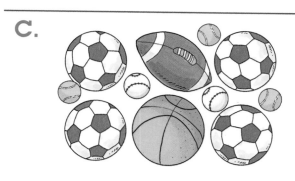

D.
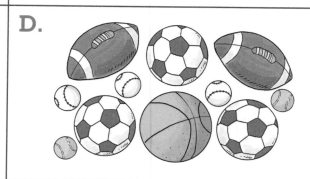

E.

F.
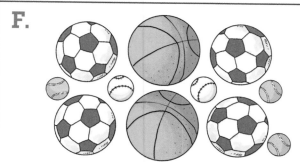

Go for the Goal!

Can you help Arthur weave his way around the field to score the winning goal? Go, Arthur, go!

START!

GOAL!

Baseball Search

It's baseball season! Help the Busytown Bugles warm up for the game by finding all of the baseball words in the puzzle below. Look across and down.

Word Bank

BALL
BASE
BAT
CAP
GLOVE
HIT
OUT
RUN
SWING

B	S	W	I	N	G	
A	L	B	A	L	L	
S	C	A	P	O	O	
E	W	T	O	L	V	
Y	W	R	U	N	E	
O	H	I	T	R	M	

What Comes Next?

Draw a line from the dot at the end of each line to the shape that comes next in the pattern. Lowly did the first one for you. Thanks, Lowly!

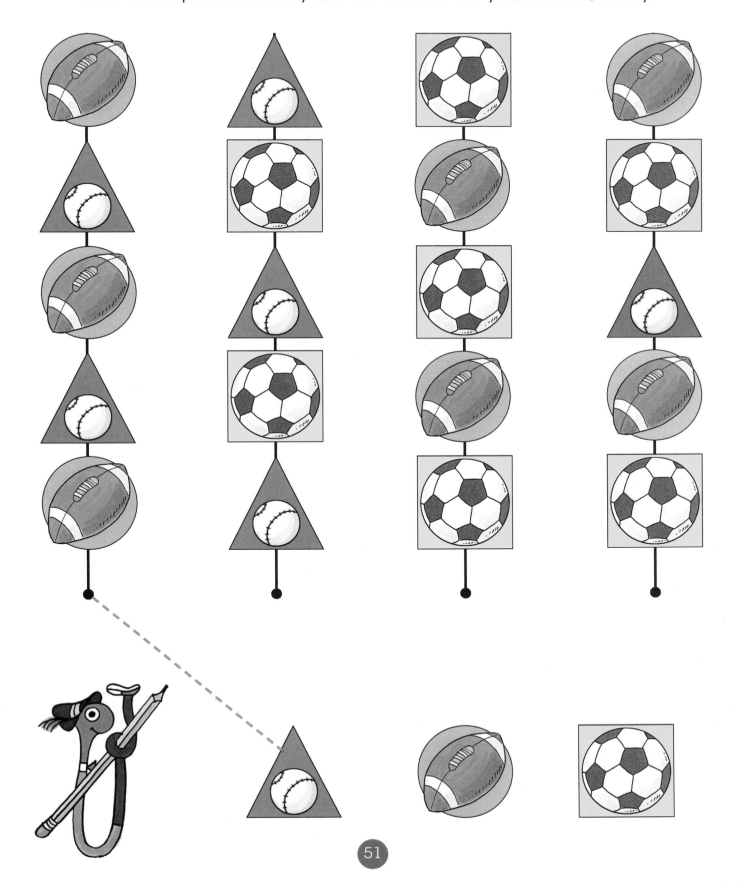

Field Goal Goldbug

Goldbug is going for the extra point! Connect the dots from 1 to 23 to help him out. Then finish coloring the picture.

Double Dribble

Can you find the 4 ways the picture on the bottom differs from the one on the top?

Party Time

It's Lowly's birthday! Help him get to his party on time!

START!

FINISH!

Mystery Gift

What present did Skip give to Lowly? Color the letters **W-O-W** in
the puzzle below, and the remaining letters will reveal the answer.
Then draw the gift outside of the box. Hurry, it's getting away!

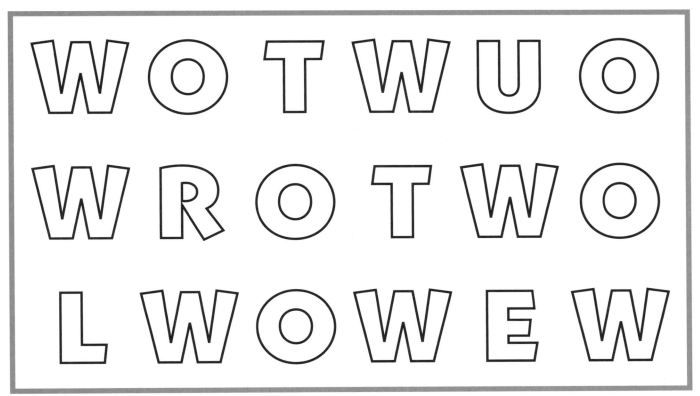

W O T W U O
W R O T W O
L W O W E W

Bunches of Balloons

Arthur brought the balloons to Lowly's party. Can you find the bunch below that has the exact same balloons that Arthur is holding?

A.

B.

C.

D.

E.

F.

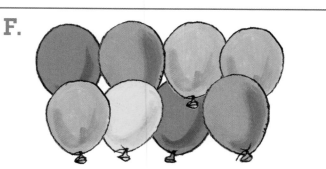

Birthday Bash

Everyone is having a great time at Lowly's party! Can you fill in the puzzle below using the picture clues? Look at the Word Bank if you need help.

1) across

2) down

4) down

5) across

6) down

3) down

7) across

Word Bank

BALLOONS

CAKE

CLOWN

FRIENDS

GAMES

GIFTS

HATS

Party Puzzle

Complete the party scene below by writing the number of each missing piece into the correct empty space. The first one is done for you.

Happy Birthday, Lowly!

Where's Lowly's cake? Connect the dots from 1 to 19 to make one for him.
Then finish coloring the picture. What should Lowly wish for?

Going to Town

Mother Cat is taking Huckle and Sally into town. Can you find the 8 ways the picture on the right is different from the one on the left?

Shopping Scramble

Oh, no! Arthur mixed up the grocery list! Help him unscramble the names of the items on the list. Use the Word Bank if you need help.

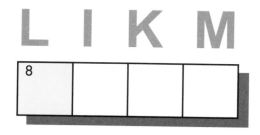

L I K M

| 8 | | | |

C E I J U

| | | | 4 | |

G E S G

| 3 | | | |

S E E C H E

| 2 | | 6 | | | |

U T F R I

| | 5 | | 1 | |

R E D A B

| | | | 7 | |

Word Bank

BREAD	FRUIT
CHEESE	JUICE
EGGS	MILK

When you are finished, write the letters found in the numbered yellow spaces into the boxes below to help Arthur remember the last item on the list.

| 1 | 2 | 3 |

| 4 | 5 | 6 | 7 | 8 |

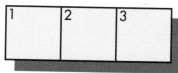

62

Produce Patterns

Arthur loves to look at all of the colorful fruit at the market. Complete these patterns by drawing the fruit that comes next at the end of each row.

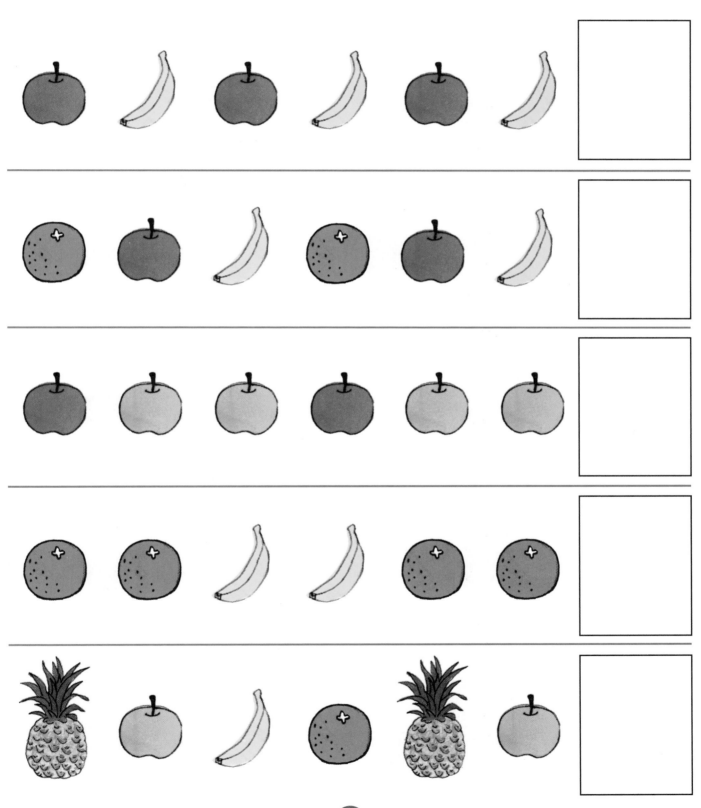

Flowers for Molly

Ella wants to make Molly a bouquet of flowers just like hers. Can you find the bunch below that has the exact same flowers that Ella is holding?
Look for the same colors, kinds, and number of flowers.

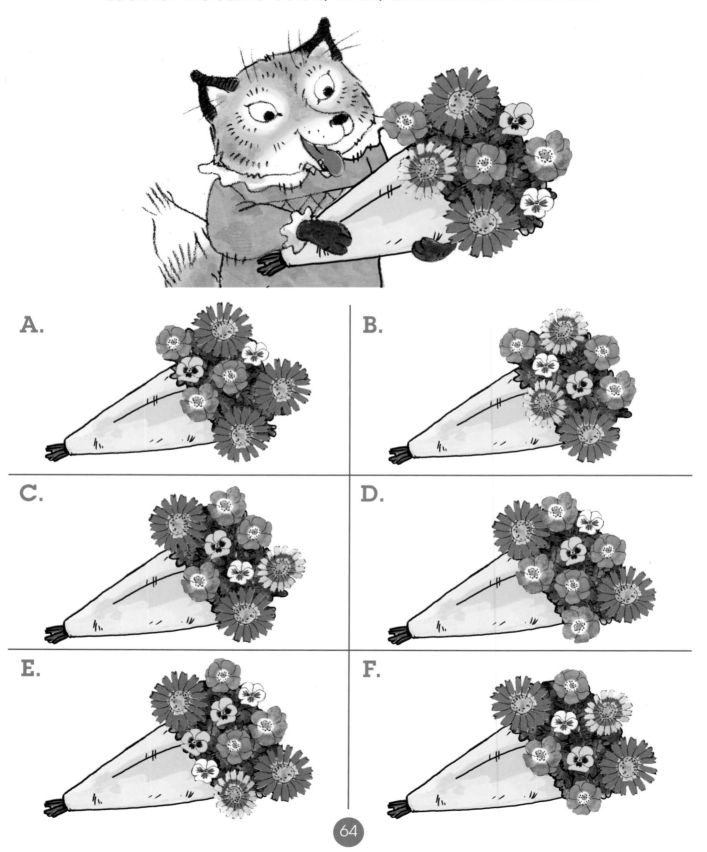

A.

B.

C.

D.

E.

F.

Color-By-Number

What are the garden bugs growing? Fill in each numbered space with the corresponding color to find out.

 1 = yellow
 2 = blue
 3 = green
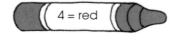 4 = red

Let's Go to the Farm

It's harvest time on Farmer Fox's farm. Can you find the 8 ways the picture on the right is different from the one on the left?

Apple Pickin'

Object of the Game
Try to form boxes by connecting dots.

Setting Up
This game is for 2 to 4 players. Each player should have a different colored pen or crayon.

How Do You Play?
1) Each player takes a turn connecting 2 neighboring dots with a straight line. You can go up and down and side to side, but not diagonally.

2) Try to be the player who makes a box by adding the last line of a square. When you do, write your initial in the box and take another turn. Each plain square is worth 1 point, each red apple is worth 2 points, and each green apple is worth 3 points!

How Do You Win?
The player with the most points wins!

2 points   **3 points**

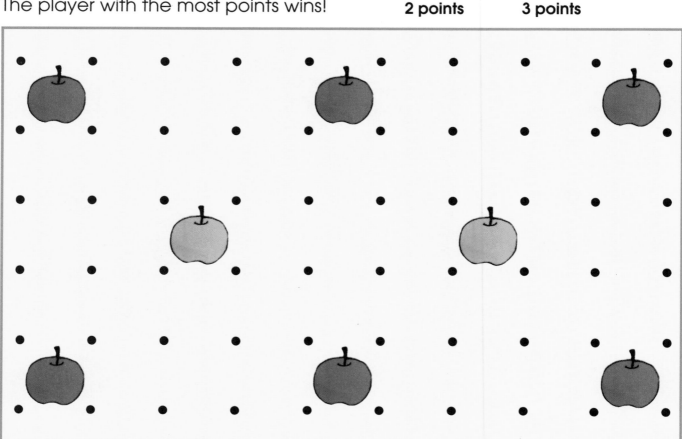

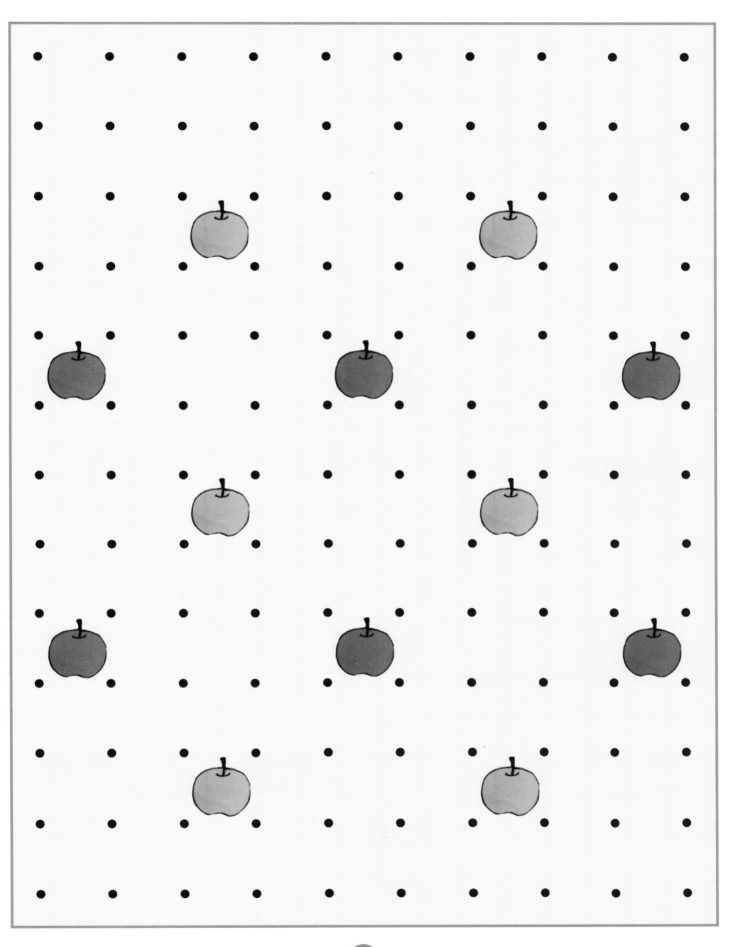

Barnyard Crossword

Huckle has many friends on the farm. Can you fill in the puzzle below using the picture clues? Look at the Word Bank in case you need help.

2) across

1) down

3) down

4) across

6) across

8) across

5) down

7) down

Word Bank

CHICKEN	GOOSE
COW	HORSE
DUCK	PIG
GOAT	SHEEP

Chicken Chase

CLUCK! CLUCK! One of Farmer Alfalfa's chickens got loose! Don't worry, Huckle can catch her! With your help, of course!

START!

FINISH!

Safari Search

Where did all of the animals go? Can you find them hiding in the puzzle below? Look across and down.

M	O	N	K	E	Y
P	A	R	R	O	T
A	E	L	T	K	O
N	M	I	I	O	U
D	U	O	G	A	C
A	H	N	E	L	A
Z	E	B	R	A	N

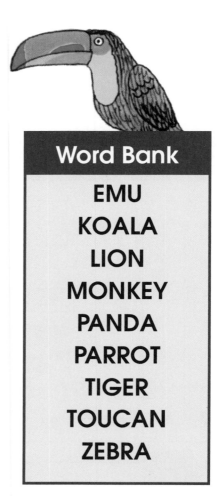

Word Bank

EMU
KOALA
LION
MONKEY
PANDA
PARROT
TIGER
TOUCAN
ZEBRA

What Comes Next?

Draw a line from the dot at the end of each line to the shape that comes next in the pattern. Lowly did the first one for you. Thanks, Lowly!

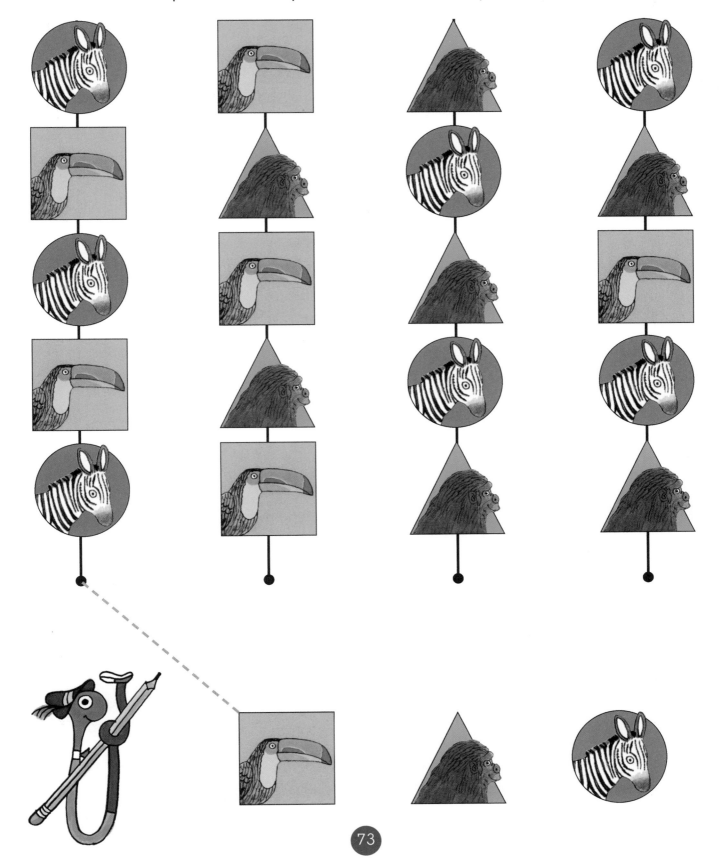

Elephant Fun

Use the secret code below to learn the answer to Lowly's joke.

Why don't elephants like to play cards?

_____ _____ _____ _____ _____ _____ _____

_____ _____ _____ _____ _____ _____ _____ _____

        !

_____ _____ _____ _____ _____ _____ _____ _____ !

A B C E F

H L O S T U

Giraffe Match

See if you can find 2 giraffes that look exactly alike.

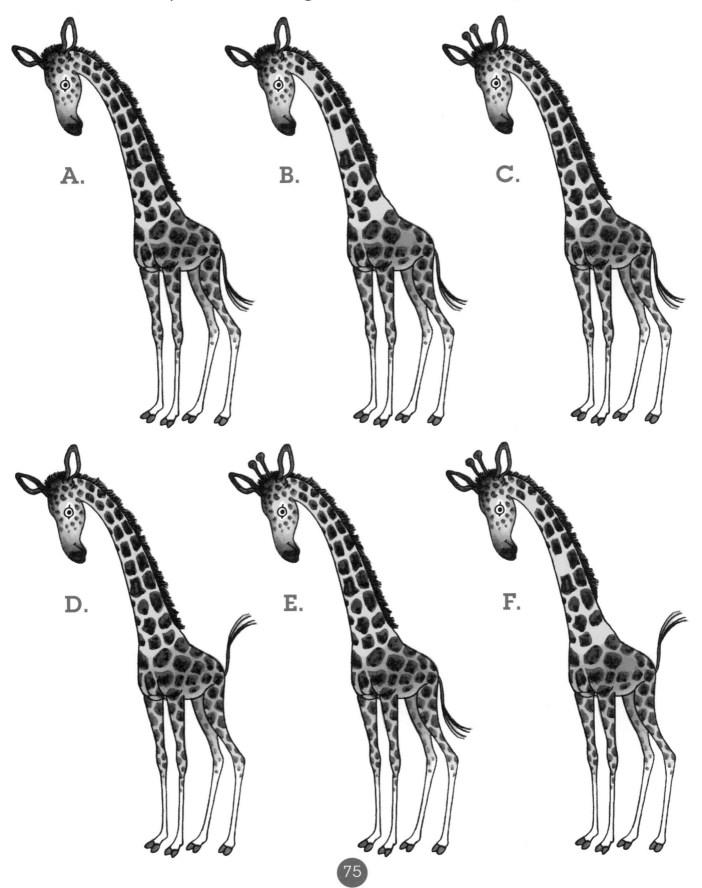

A.

B.

C.

D.

E.

F.

Crazy Planes!

The Crazy Planes are having fun looping through the sky. Use the **green deck** of cards to play a fun game with them!

Object of the Game

Be the first player to get rid of all of the cards in your hand.

Setting Up

This game is for 2 to 4 players.
The green deck contains 40 vehicle cards.

- Shuffle the cards.
- The dealer deals 5 cards facedown to each player.
- Place the rest of the deck facedown in the center of the table. Turn the top card over and place it next to the pile. This will be the discard pile.
- If the first card flipped over is an **8** (a "Crazy Planes" card), shuffle it back into the pile and flip over another card.

How Do You Play?

1) The player to the left of the dealer plays first. She must take one card from her hand and place it face up on the discard pile. This card must match either the **color** or the **number** of the card on top of the pile. For example:

If the top card on the discard pile is number 1 and orange ...

... then you can play another number 1 card of any color ...

... or you can play another orange card with any other number.

2) All of the **8** cards are "Crazy Planes" and wild cards. They can be played at any time and do not need to match another number or color.

3) After a player puts down a Crazy Plane card, she gets to say which color the next player has to put down.

4) After a player makes her move, play continues with the player to the left.

5) A player who cannot match the color or number of a card or use a Crazy Plane card must draw a card from the draw pile. She must keep drawing cards one at a time until she is able to make a play.

6) If all of the cards in the draw pile are gone and the player still cannot play, it is the next player's turn.

How Do You Win?
Be the first player to get rid of all of your cards!

You can also use this deck of cards to play the Hide-and-Seek game on page 17!

Who's at the Zoo?

What animal do Huckle and Lowly see at the zoo? Color any letters that appear more than 3 times in the puzzle below. The leftover letters will reveal the answer. Then draw the animal!

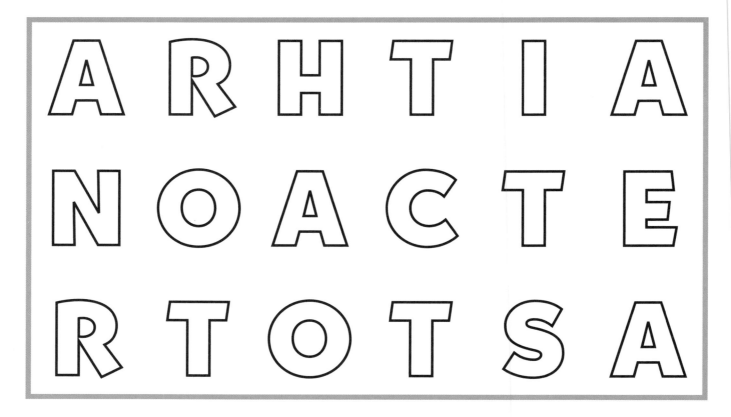

A R H T I A
N O A C T E R
R T O T S A

Color-By-Number

What is hiding up in the tree? Fill in each numbered space with the corresponding color to find out.

1 = yellow

2 = blue

3 = red

4 = green

5 = brown

6 = black

It's OK to leave the spaces with no number white!

Treasure Trail

Shiver me timbers! The pirates are looking for treasure, but the map is damaged. Can you put the 3 missing pieces in the right places to complete the pathway to the treasure?

START!

FINISH!

Pirate Adventure Board Game

These are the rules and instructions for the board game on the next two pages. You can keep the game board inside the book, or tear the pages out along the perforations and tape them together.

Object of the Game
Help Huckle and his band of pirates find the buried treasure.

Setting Up
- 2 to 4 players
- 4 coins (any kind will do!)
- A game piece for each player (cut out from page 96)

How Do You Play?
1) Each player drops the four coins. The one with the greatest number of heads goes first, the second-greatest number of heads goes second, and so on. Each player puts his game token at the START.

2) When it is your turn, drop the 4 coins. The number of heads you get is the number of spaces you can move your game token along the path to the Treasure Chest.

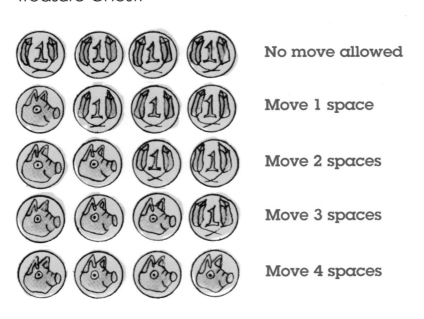

	No move allowed
	Move 1 space
	Move 2 spaces
	Move 3 spaces
	Move 4 spaces

When you're ready to play, turn the page! Yo, ho, ho!

3) When you land on a space with writing on it, do what it says.

How Do You Win?
The first player to get to the Treasure Chest wins! X marks the spot!

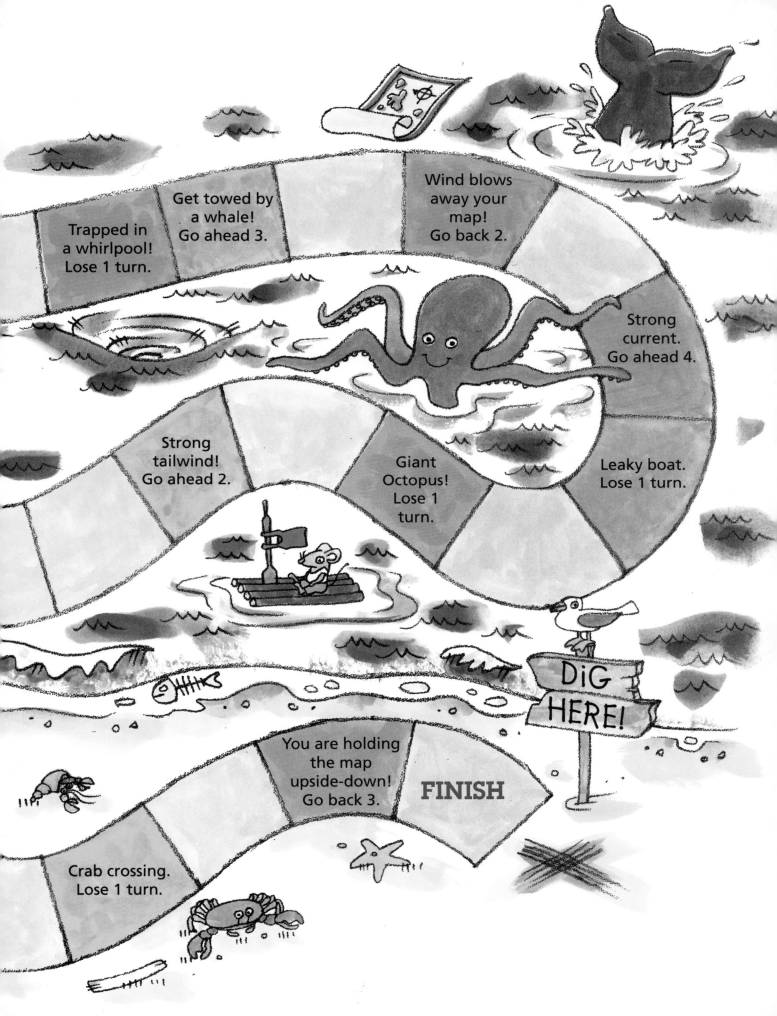

Wintery World

It's wintertime in Busytown. Can you find 6 things
that do not belong in the winter scene below?

Who's There?

Connect the dots from 1 to 45 to see what Lowly
is making in the snow. Then color the picture.

Let It Snow!

Summer is great, but there's lots of things to do in winter, too! Can you find the 8 ways the picture on the right is different from the one on the left?

Card Search

Huckle and Bridget love to play cards. See if you can find the card-themed words from the Word Bank in the puzzle below. Look across and down. Then circle the leftover letters to find the hidden word!

```
D I D Q H A
A C E U E S
M O C E A P
J O K E R A
A N D N T D
C L U B S E
K I N G S S
```

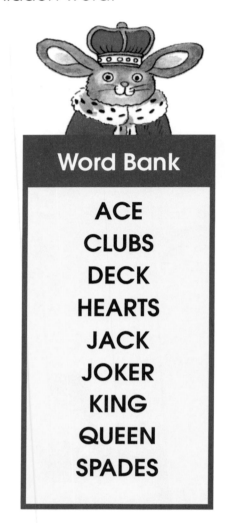

Word Bank

ACE
CLUBS
DECK
HEARTS
JACK
JOKER
KING
QUEEN
SPADES

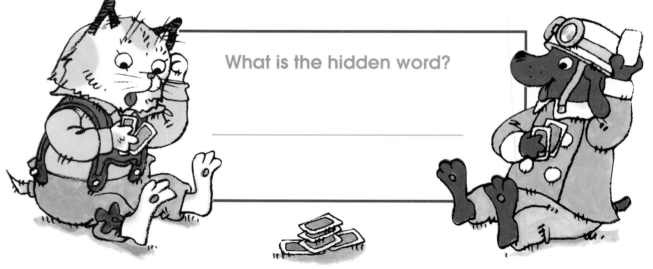

What is the hidden word?

_____

What Comes Next?

Complete these patterns of cards by circling the one that comes next at the end of each row.

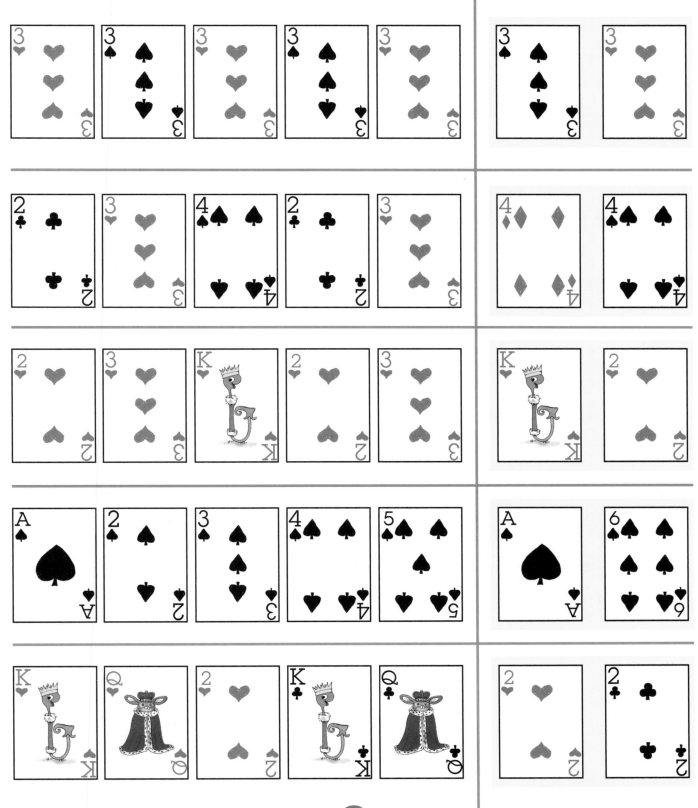

Answers (Just in case you need help!)

An Airborne Adventure! pp. 4-5

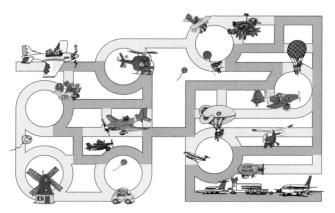

Let's Go to the Air Show pp. 6-7

1) The hat of the pilot in the yellow plane is on his head.
2) The star on the wing of the green plane is missing.
3) There is a parachuting bug.
4) The small white plane is facing to the right.
5) The yellow balloon is replaced with a red one.
6) The smile face on the side of the dog pilot's plane is replaced with a target.
7) The mice on the wing of the larger white plane are missing.
8) The small yellow plane on the ground has been replaced with a pink one.

Bicycle Search p. 8

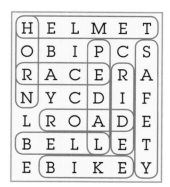

Let's Roll p. 9

PLAYGROUND

Two-Wheeler p. 10

C and E are the same.

Roadwork p. 11

What Doesn't Belong? p. 12

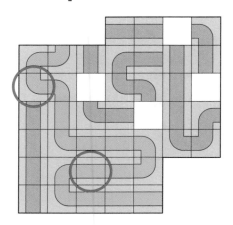

Picnic Panic! p. 13

Camping Crossword p. 14

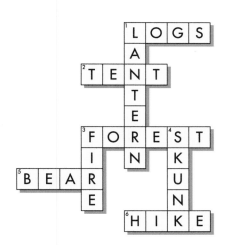

Crossword grid:
- 1 across: LOGS
- 1 down: LANTERN
- 2 across: TENT
- 3 across: FOREST
- 3 down: FIRE
- 4 down: SKUNK
- 5 across: BEARE
- 6 across: HIKE

What Comes Next? p. 25

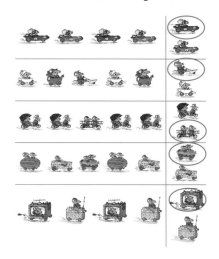

Lost! pp. 18-19

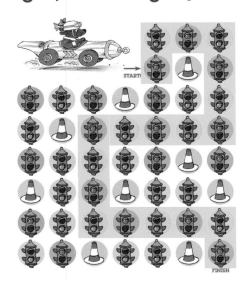

Go, Huckle, Go! p. 20

B and F are the same.

Red Light, Green Light p. 24

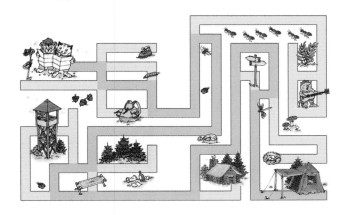

Let's Go to the Museum pp. 26-27

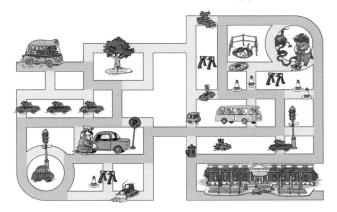

Fossil Find p. 28

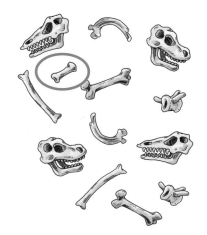

Sandbox Search p. 30

Word search grid:

T	R	O	C	K	S
R	D	I	G	P	H
U	S	X	C	L	O
C	A	R	S	A	V
K	N	N	I	Y	E
S	D	P	A	I	L

Fun and Games p. 31

What Comes Next? p. 37

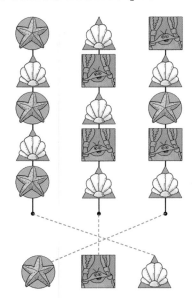

A Fair Day pp. 32-33

1) The red balloon in the sky is missing.
2) There is a bear on the swing ride.
3) The train is going in the other direction.
4) The orange and yellow flag is different.
5) The red, green, and blue flag is different.
6) There is a mother rabbit and her child standing near the roller coaster instead of a pig.
7) The mouse to the left of the balloon man is different.
8) The mouse to the right of the balloon man has 1 balloon instead of 3.

Let's Go to the Seashore p. 38

Sea Search p. 42

Summertime p. 36

Marine Mystery p. 43

OCTOPUS

Seaside Scene p. 44

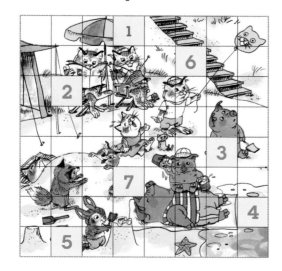

Tacklebox Tangle p. 45

A-2   B-3   C-1

Sports Stuff p. 48

D has the same kinds of balls.

Go for the Goal! p. 49

Baseball Search p. 50

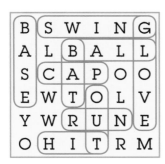

What Comes Next? p. 51

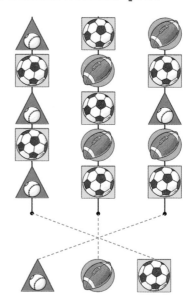

Double Dribble p. 53

1) Ella is not peeking over the wall.
2) The small tree branch is missing.
3) Frances's hair bow is missing.
4) Arthur is peeking out from behind the tree.

Party Time p. 54

Mystery Gift p. 55

TURTLE

Bunches of Balloons p. 56

E matches Arthur's balloons.

Birthday Bash p. 57

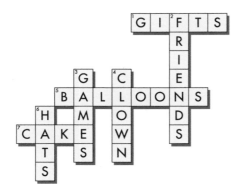

Party Puzzle p. 58

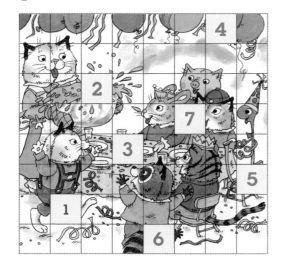

Going to Town pp. 60-61

1) There are 2 smokestacks on the building on the left.
2) There is someone in the third window of the building on the left.
3) There is a submarine car instead of a taxi.
4) The mouse is looking out of a different window of the building on the right.
5) There is a dog looking out of the left window of the building on the right.
6) A potted tree on the left of the bank is missing.
7) The blue car is going in the other direction.
8) There is a trash can in front of the building on the right.

Shopping Scramble p. 62

LIKM = MILK   SEECHE = CHEESE
CEIJU = JUICE   UTFRI = FRUIT
GESG = EGGS   REDAB = BREAD

The last item on the list:
ICE CREAM

Produce Patterns p. 63

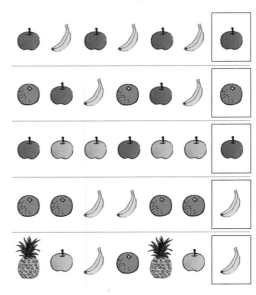

Flowers for Molly p. 64

F matches Ella's bouquet.

Let's Go to the Farm pp. 66-67

1) The person at the top of the tree is wearing a different hat.
2) There is a barn in the background instead of a house.
3) One of the apples on the left side of the tree is missing.
4) There is a small pumpkin next to the hay on the left.
5) The white hen is replaced with a chick.
6) There are 3 candy apples instead of 4.
7) The farm stand has grape juice instead of apple juice.
8) There is a face on the large pumpkin.

Barnyard Crossword p. 70

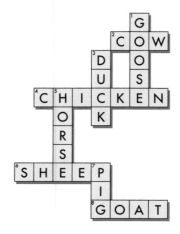

Chicken Chase p. 71

Safari Search p. 72

What Comes Next? p. 73

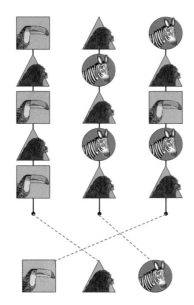

Elephant Fun p. 74

Q: Why don't elephants like to play cards?
A: BECAUSE OF ALL THE CHEETAHS!

Giraffe Match p. 75

C and E are the same.

Who's at the Zoo? p. 78

RHINOCEROS

Treasure Trail p. 80

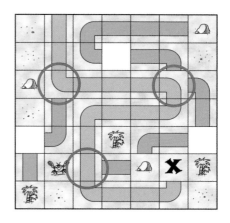

Wintery World p. 84

Game Tokens

Ask a grown-up to help you cut out the game pieces below!

Use these tokens for the **Busytown Race Game** found on pages 22-23.

Use these tokens for the **Pirate Adventure Game** found on pages 82-83.

Keep your game tokens in the pocket at the back of this book!

Let It Snow! pp. 86-87

1) The helicopter is flying in the other direction.
2) The clock is showing a different time.
3) The snowman has a different hat.
4) Huckle's hat is green instead of red.
5) The skier fell in the snow.
6) There is a mouse pushing a snowball.
7) There are 2 cabins in the background instead of 1.
8) The ice skater on the left is going in a different direction.

Card Search p. 88

The hidden word is DIAMONDS

What Comes Next? p. 89

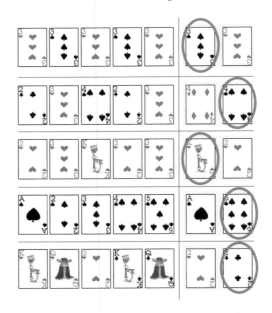

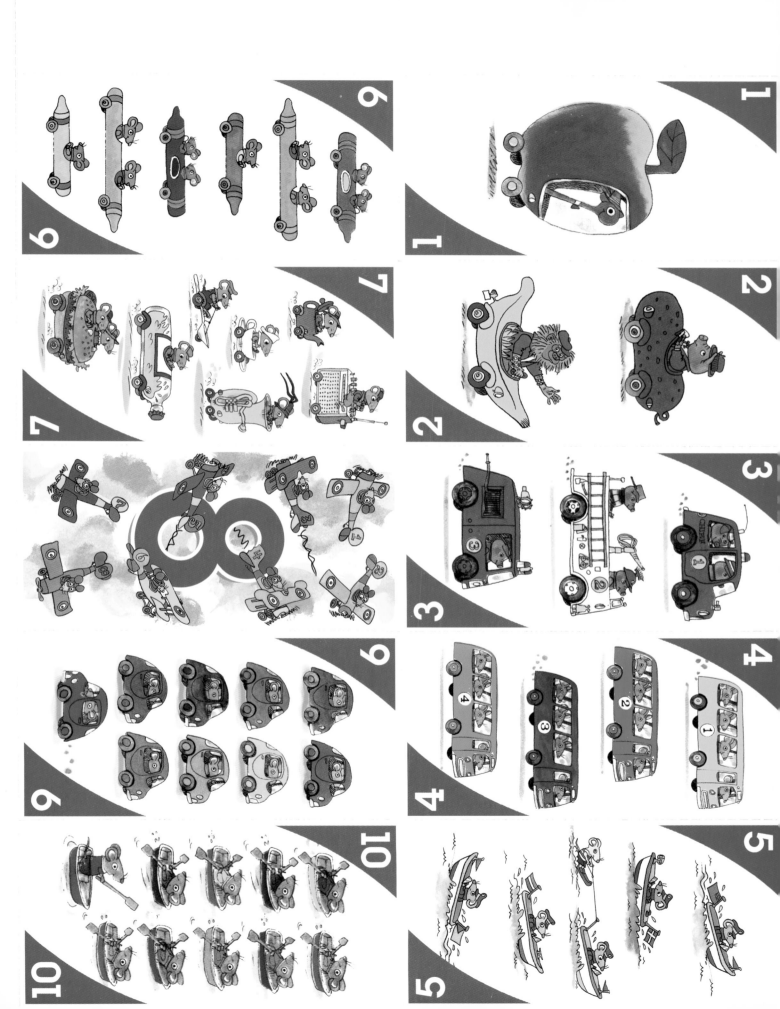

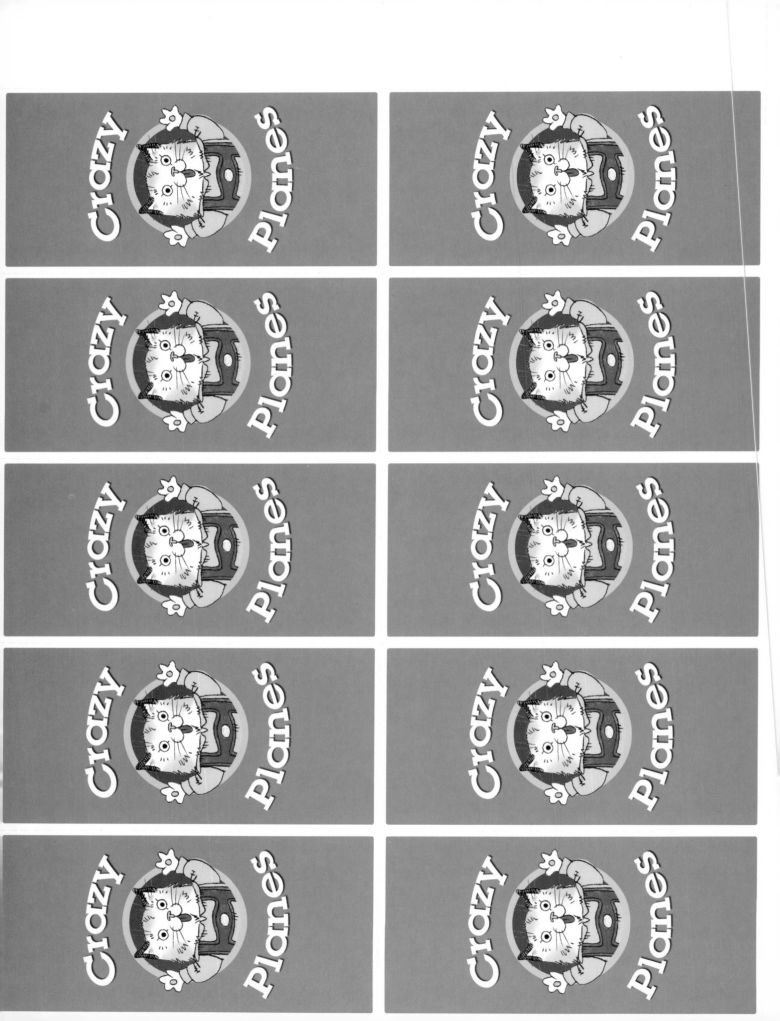

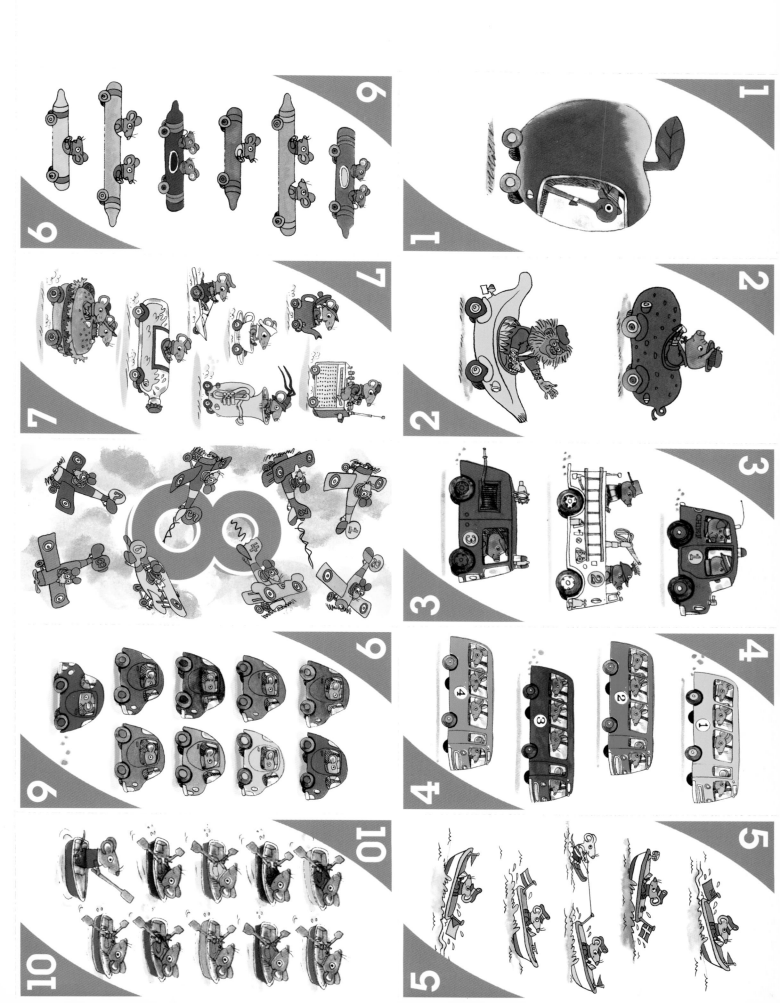

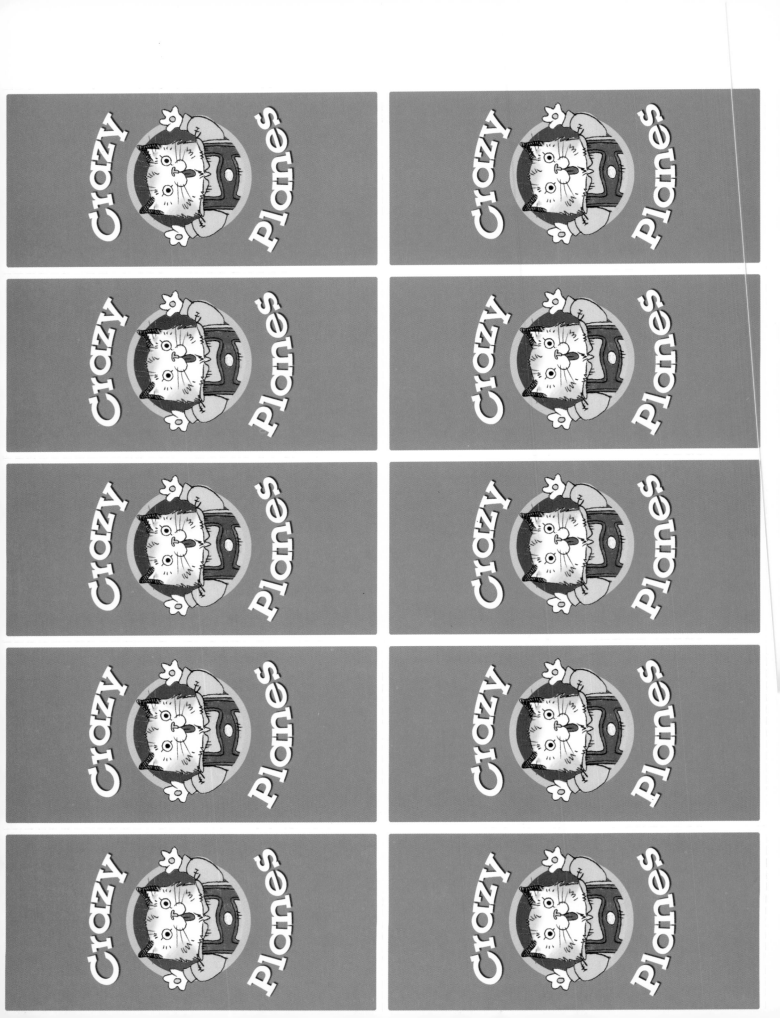

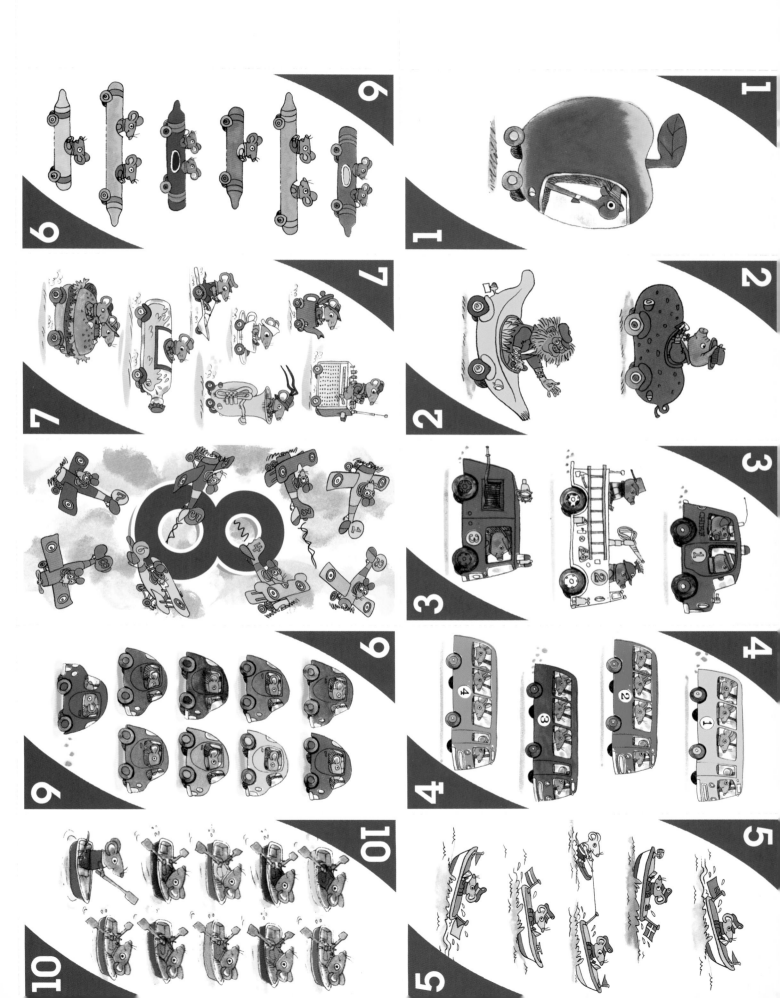

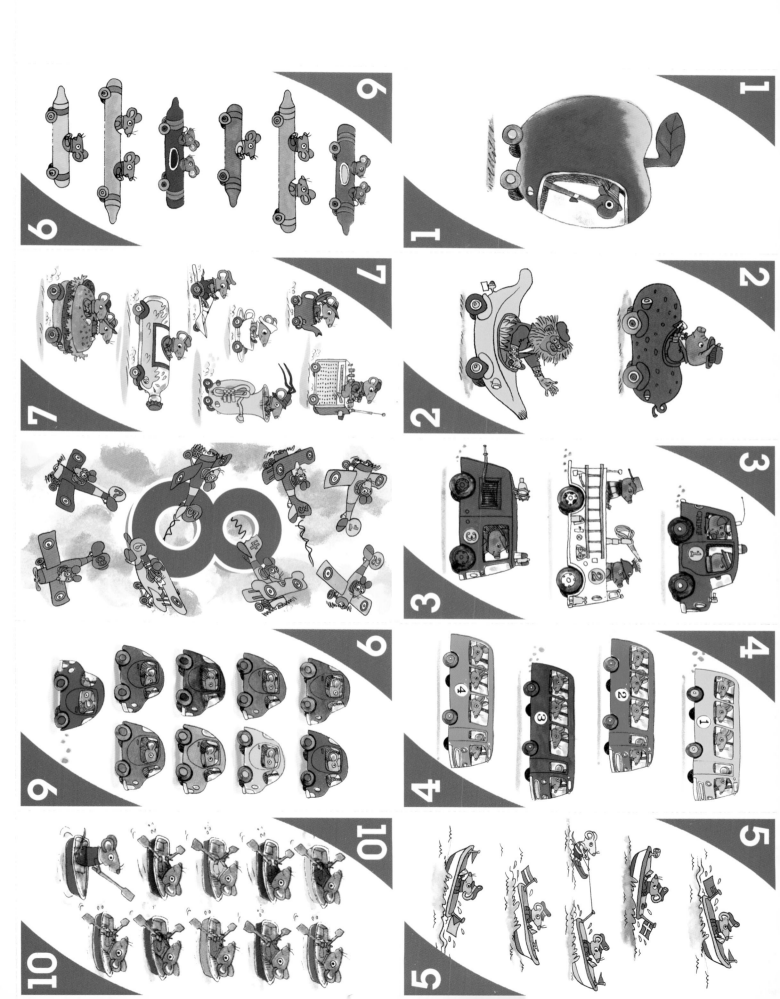

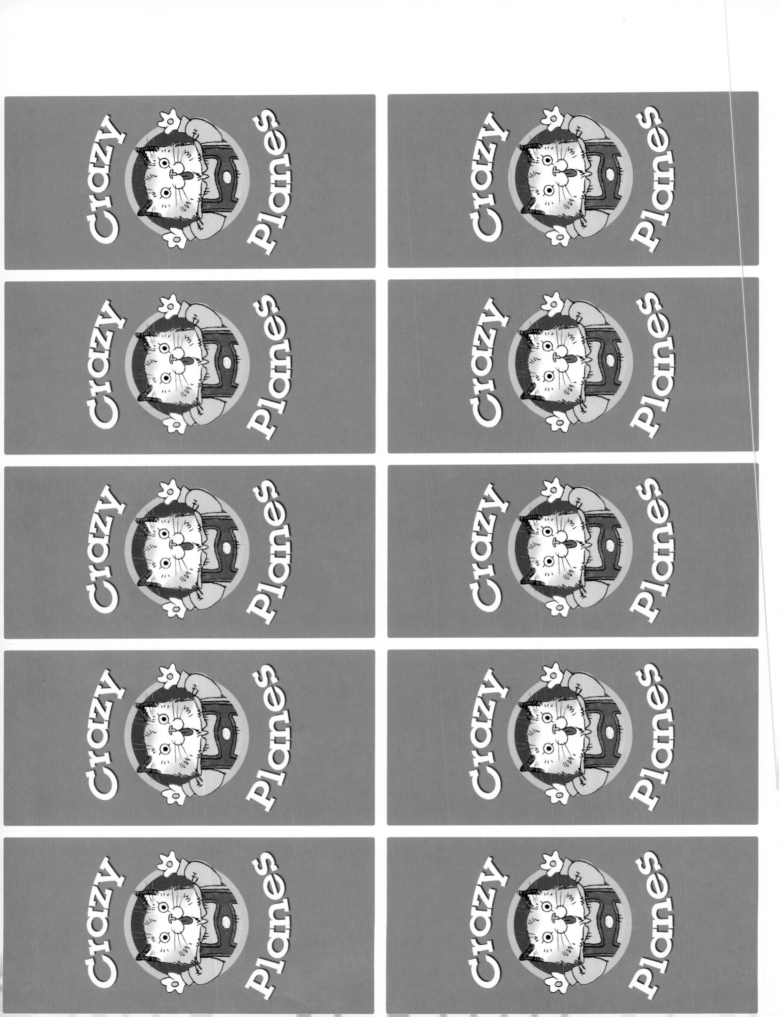

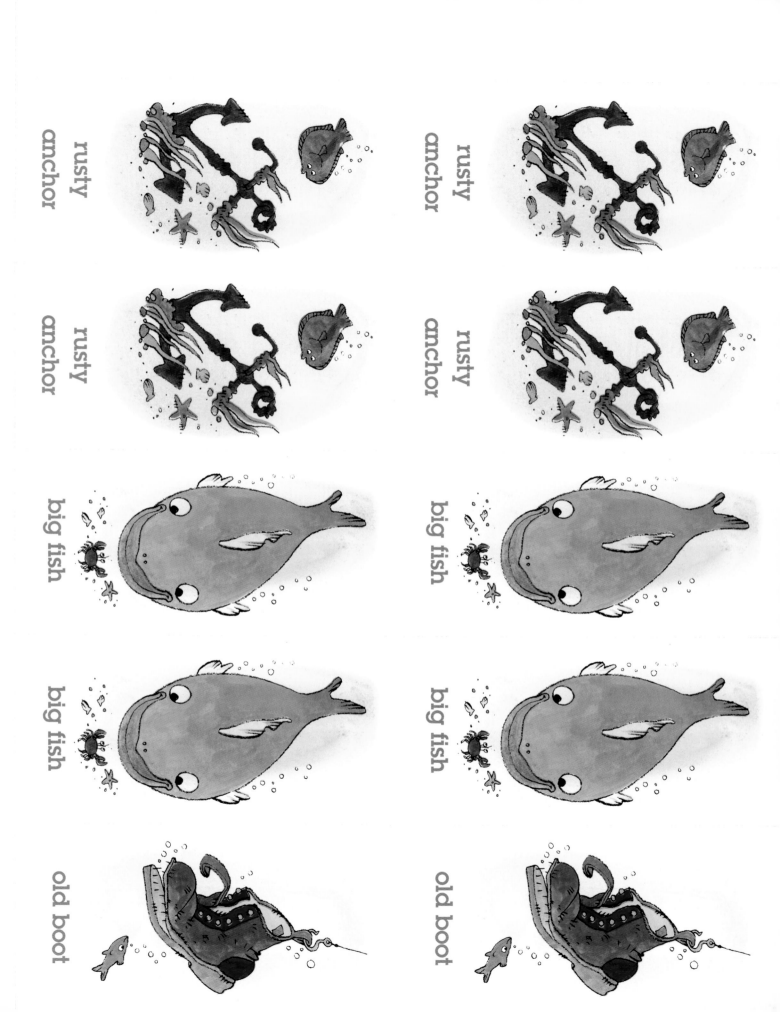

rusty
anchor

rusty
anchor

big fish

big fish

old boot

rusty
anchor

rusty
anchor

big fish

big fish

old boot

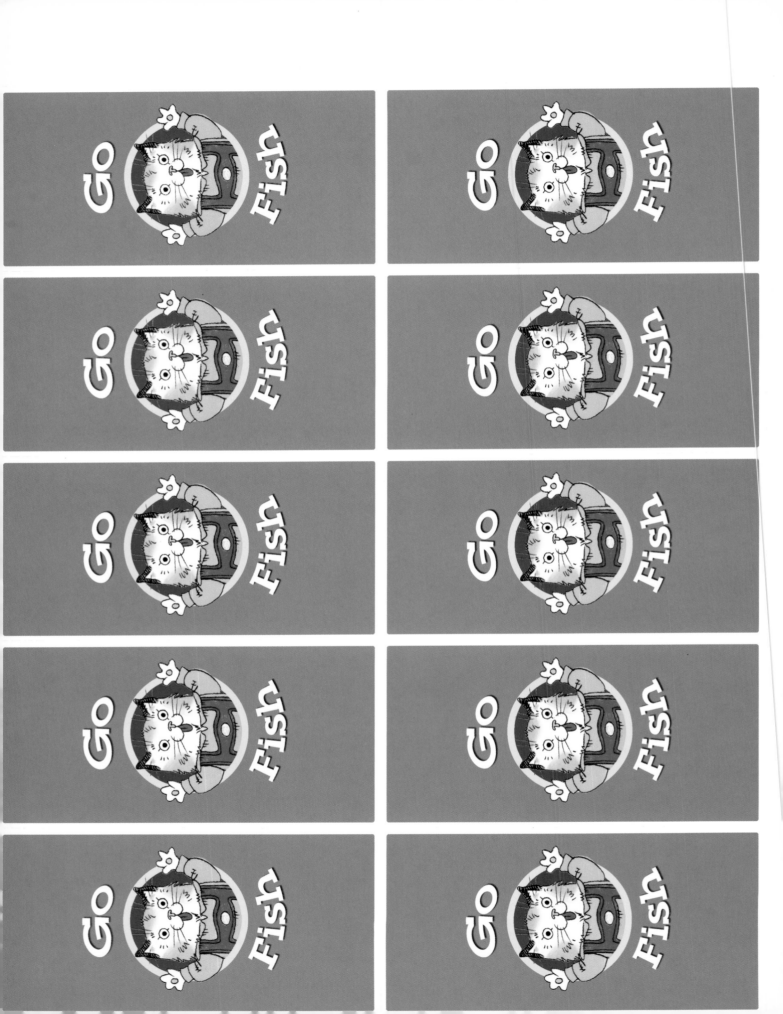

message
in a bottle

message
in a bottle

tin can

tin can

old boot

message
in a bottle

message
in a bottle

tin can

tin can

old boot

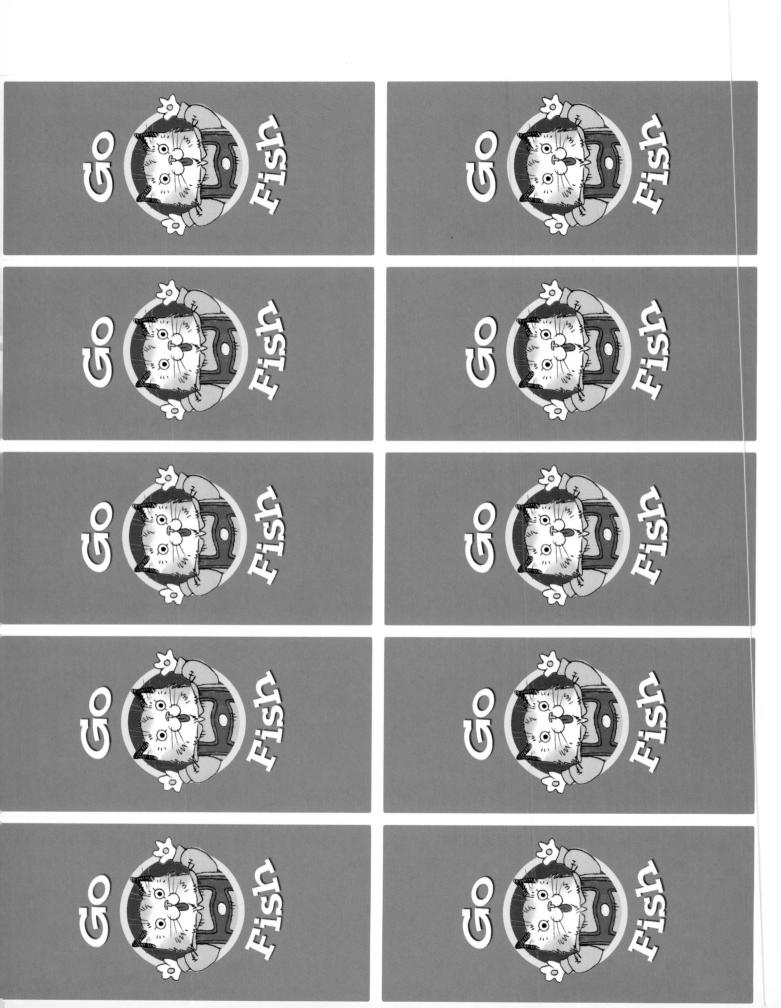

treasure
chest

treasure
chest

little fish

little fish

spare
tire

treasure
chest

treasure
chest

little fish

little fish

spare
tire

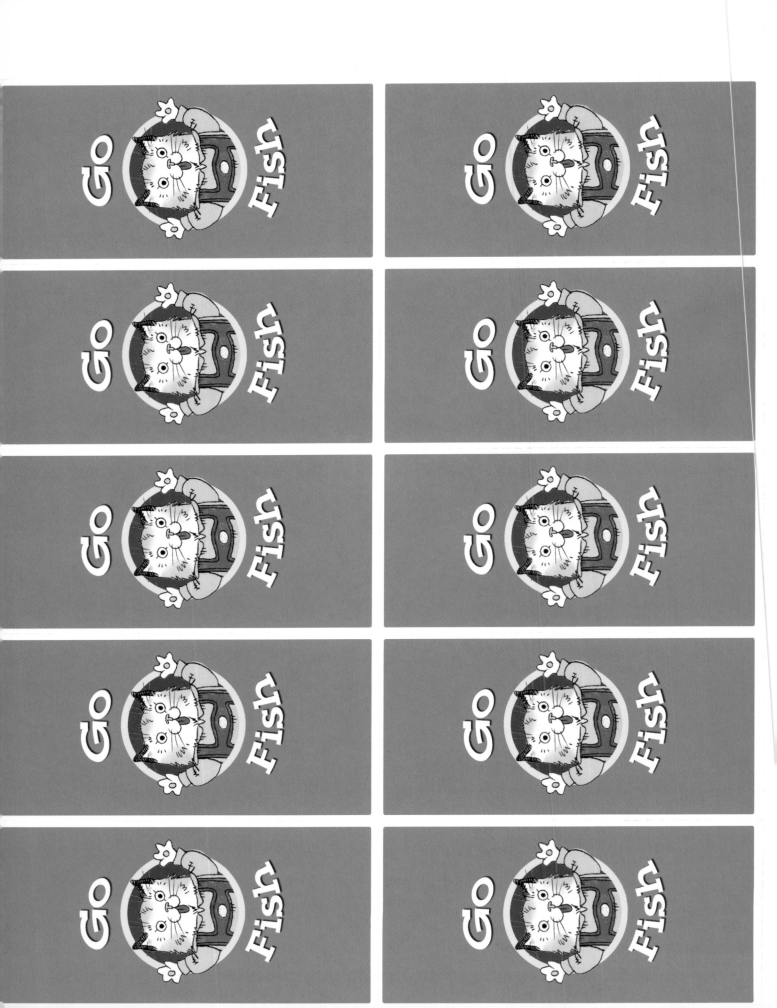

spare
tire

ship's
wheel

ship's
wheel

Lowly
Worm

Arthur
Pig

spare
tire

ship's
wheel

ship's
wheel

Lowly
Worm

Arthur
Pig

Bridget
Murphy

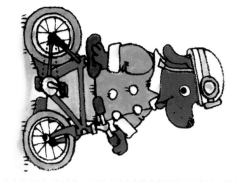

Bridget
Murphy

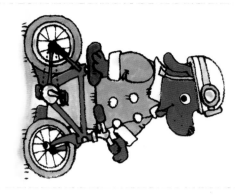

Sean
Sheep

Sean
Sheep

Ella
Fox

Ella
Fox

Frances
Raccoon

Frances
Raccoon

Goldbug

Goldbug

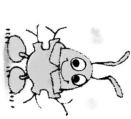

Huckle
Cat

Jimmy
Crocodile

Mildred
Hippo

Molly
Rabbit

Sally
Cat

Huckle
Cat

Jimmy
Crocodile

Mildred
Hippo

Molly
Rabbit

Sally
Cat

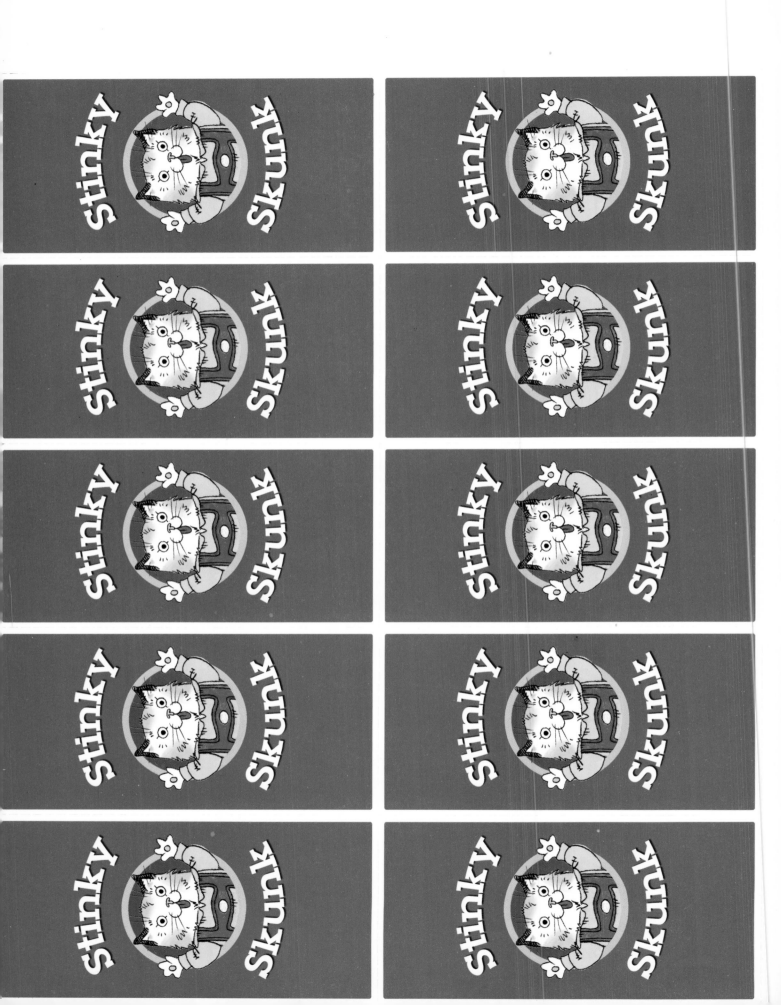

Skip
Tiger

Squeaky
Mouse

Ursula
Pig

Victor
Bear

Skip
Tiger

Squeaky
Mouse

Ursula
Pig

Victor
Bear

Stinky
Skunk

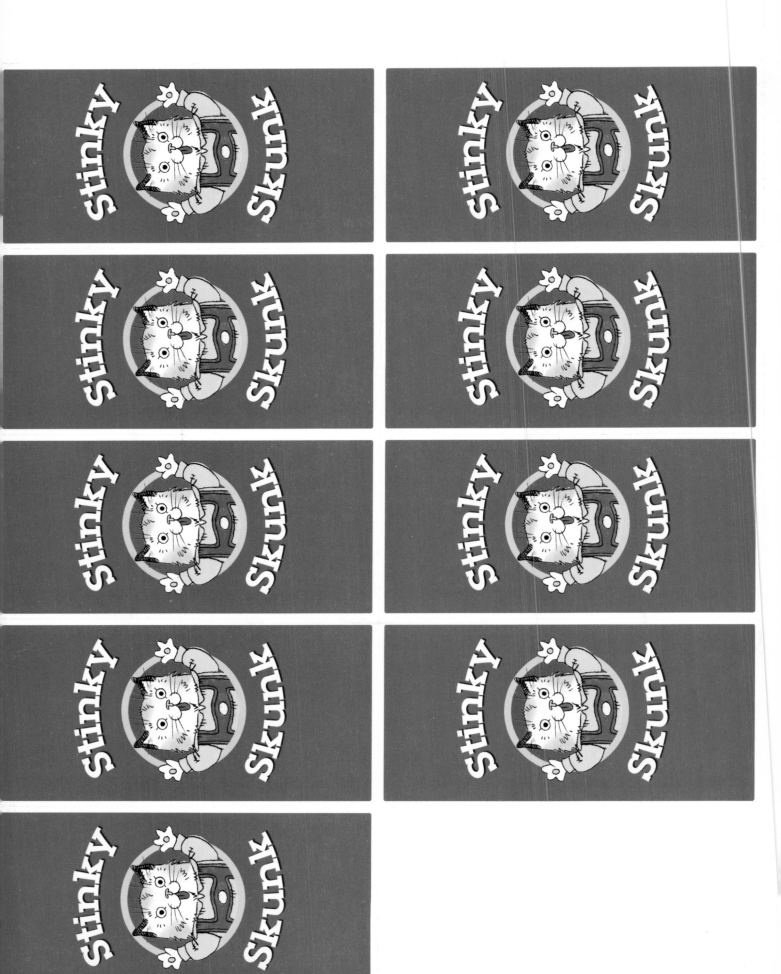